8/10

The Universal Declaration of Human Rights

MILESTONES
IN MODERN
WORLD HISTORY

1600 · · · 1750 · · ·   · · 1940 · · · 2000

The Bolshevik Revolution

The Chinese Cultural
Revolution

The Collapse of
the Soviet Union

D-Day and the Liberation
of France

The End of Apartheid
in South Africa

The Iranian Revolution

The Treaty of Versailles

The Universal Declaration
of Human Rights

MILESTONES
IN MODERN
WORLD HISTORY

1600 · · · 1750 · ·   · · · · 1940 · · · 2000

The Universal Declaration of Human Rights

SUSAN MUADDI DARRAJ

CHELSEA HOUSE
PUBLISHERS
An imprint of Infobase Publishing

The Universal Declaration of Human Rights

Chelsea House
An imprint of Infobase Publishing
132 West 31st Street
New York, NY 10001

Library of Congress Cataloging-in-Publication Data

Darraj, Susan Muaddi.
The Universal Declaration of Human Rights / Susan Muaddi Darraj.
  p. cm. — (Milestones in modern world history)
Includes bibliographical references and index.
ISBN 978-1-60413-494-0 (hardcover)
1. United Nations. General Assembly. Universal Declaration of Human
Rights—History. 2. Human rights—History. I. Title.
K3238.31948.D37 2009
341.4'8—dc22   2009003663

Chelsea House books are available at special discounts when purchased in bulk quantities for businesses, associations, institutions, or sales promotions. Please call our Special Sales Department in New York at (212) 967-8800 or (800) 322-8755.

You can find Chelsea House on the World Wide Web at http://www.chelseahouse.com.

Text design by Erik Lindstrom
Cover design by Alicia Post
Composition by Keith Trego
Cover printed by Bang Printing, Brainerd, MN
Book printed and bound by Bang Printing, Brainerd, MN
Date printed: January 2010
Printed in the United States of America

10 9 8 7 6 5 4 3 2 1

This book is printed on acid-free paper.

All links and Web addresses were checked and verified to be correct at the time of publication. Because of the dynamic nature of the Web, some addresses and links may have changed since publication and may no longer be valid.

CONTENTS

First Lady
of the World

A PHONE CALL

In the winter of 1945, Eleanor Roosevelt, the widow of former President Franklin Delano Roosevelt, received a phone call from her husband's successor, President Harry Truman. He was about to ask her to serve a very important role for the United States.

The current president had served as her husband's vice president and taken over his duties when Roosevelt died in office earlier that year, on April 12. Eleanor Roosevelt had been very active in her husband's administration, which was the longest of any American president: FDR had been elected to four terms in office, serving from 1933 to 1945. Throughout his political career, his wife had aided him tremendously, especially after he had developed polio in 1921, a debilitating disease that left him paralyzed. During his presidency, Eleanor Roosevelt had helped him manage White House affairs, made speeches on his behalf, and handled other important tasks for her husband. In doing so, she proved herself to be a capable, diplomatic, and effective stateswoman.

Since her husband died, Eleanor Roosevelt had kept up a correspondence with President Truman, sharing with him her thoughts on many issues and even questioning some of his decisions. Her biographer Lois Scharf notes, "Harry Truman found her counsel was often wise but also unremitting and even irritating."[1] He could not, however, dismiss a woman of her stature, experience, and popularity.

During their phone conversation on this winter day, Truman asked Roosevelt to serve as one of the American delegates to the first organizational meeting of the United Nations (UN), which would be held in London, England, in January 1946. The post was significant because FDR had been a strong advocate of the establishment of a United Nations after World War II (1939–1945). In a subsequent letter to Roosevelt, Truman wrote:

> You, as a representative of the United States will bear the grave responsibility of demonstrating the wholehearted support which this government is pledged to give to the United Nations Organization, to that end that the organization can become the means of preserving the international peace and of creating conditions of mutual trust and economic and social well-being among all peoples of the world. I am confident that you will do your best to assist these purposes in the first meeting of the General Assembly.[2]

Roosevelt hesitated about accepting the position. True, she had helped her late husband in many administrative duties, and she was widely respected as a capable, intelligent woman.

Eleanor Roosevelt is photographed at Lime Grove television studios in London in April 1951, during her tenure as chair of the United Nations Commission on Human Rights. The former first lady would have a powerful influence in shaping the Universal Declaration of Human Rights.

However, she worried that she did not possess the specific talents that such a position would demand. Scharf notes Eleanor had little reason to doubt herself: "She firmly held to the ideals of international cooperation for which the new United Nations Organization held great promise, and she had honed her skills as a parliamentarian decades earlier."[3] Those closest to her urged her to take on the task, which she did. She later said that the appointment was a tribute to her late husband, as the United Nations was one of his legacies.

Truman was thrilled. Sending the former first lady as part of the U.S. delegation would signal to the world just how seriously the United States considered the formation of a strong international organization such as the United Nations. And as Scharf slyly points out, he had "discovered a post that would periodically send her abroad."[4]

"THE SAFE SPOT FOR HER"

Although Congress approved her appointment almost unanimously, some of the other delegation members—all men—were not thrilled with her selection. The other delegates included John Foster Dulles, one of the United States' most eminent statesmen at the time. A prominent political adviser who would later serve as secretary of state under President Dwight D. Eisenhower (1953–1961), Dulles keenly understood the inner workings of governments and organizational procedure. He would also be a major contributor to the drafting of the United Nations Charter.

As previously mentioned, the United Nations' first meeting was an organizational one, during which several committees were established, each charged with handling a certain area or range of issues. Committee III was established to handle educational, humanitarian, and cultural issues that the new organization would be expected to address. Roosevelt's male colleagues met privately and agreed to assign her to this committee, as opposed to the ones that would be handling issues

Pictured, some of the 500,000 German children in a refugee camp in Vienna, Austria, circa 1948. The plight of displaced persons in the postwar period was a major concern for the United Nations.

such as war, economic issues, security, weapons, and the like. Roosevelt was not pleased with the way the assignment was handled, later stating that she imagined the group of men saying to themselves: "Ah, here's the safe spot for her—Committee Three. She can't do much harm there!"[5] She did not raise a fuss, however, in order to show her willingness to work hard wherever they placed her.

Roosevelt prepared for the meeting by reading reports, briefs, and background material. She attended every committee and subcommittee meeting scheduled, making a deep impression on everyone about how seriously she took her role. And then, in an ironic twist, Committee III turned out to be where one of the most controversial issues of the January organizational meeting—refugees—ended up.

At the end of World War II, millions of people had become refugees and were placed in what were called DP (displaced person) camps. Many of these refugees were survivors of the Holocaust—the systematic, state-sponsored extermination by Nazi Germany, under Adolf Hitler, of an estimated 6 million European Jews both before and during World War II. Many Holocaust survivors' countries of origin had fallen under Soviet influence after the end of the war. These DPs feared returning to their former homes, believing that their predominantly anti-Communist views would ensure their imprisonment and even death, since many Eastern European countries now had pro-Soviet Union, pro-Communist governments.

Eleanor Roosevelt and many other Western delegates to the United Nations favored allowing the DPs to choose whether to return to their countries of origin or to resettle in a different country. Many of the delegates, Roosevelt included, agreed that forcing them to return to their country of origin was like imposing a death sentence on these people who had already suffered tremendously.

The delegates from the Soviet Union disagreed with this option, insisting that those DPs who feared returning home must be traitors to their countries. The most vocal of the Soviet delegates was their leader, Andrey Vyshinsky, a powerful, well-spoken man who served under Joseph Stalin, the autocratic leader of the Soviet Union since the early 1920s. As the chief prosecutor of the Soviet Union in the 1930s, Vyshinsky participated in the purges—long periods of terror in which Stalin had many of his political opponents executed or imprisoned.

A February 1946 photo of the Soviet legal expert and diplomat Andrey Vyshinsky. He clashed with Eleanor Roosevelt about the fate of European refugees at the United Nations.

Vyshinsky was known to be a fiery orator and skillful debater. Soon, he found himself debating the former first lady of the United States.

Dulles asked Roosevelt, as a member of Committee III, to debate Vyshinsky on the issue of displaced persons. While she believed strongly in the right of these refugees to choose to resettle in another country, she was terrified of debating Vyshinsky. She did her duty, however, and made her argument before the UN General Assembly.

Vyshinsky had argued persuasively in favor of compulsory repatriation: The DPs would be forced to return to their country of origin. His argument relied on the idea that it would be a disservice to all nations to have their citizens move elsewhere. Eleanor Roosevelt made an equally powerful counterargument: If the United Nations were to be effective internationally, it should not concern itself with nations, but with the rights of mankind. She argued that nations and governments, as all had seen during the war, changed, fell, and were recreated all the time, but the rights of individual human beings superseded national boundaries.

Her argument proved more persuasive than Vyshinsky's. The vote held on the issue favored the option of allowing DPs to choose their country of resettlement, a major victory for Roosevelt. The woman who had been shy about her lack of parliamentary skills and hesitated to join the delegation had soundly defeated one of the Soviet Union's most effective legal minds and diplomats. And she had done something more: She had established herself as a powerful advocate for the rights of human beings. Scharf writes, "She emerged from the London session as an effective spokesperson for human rights and dignity."[6]

The Aftermath
of World War II

THE FORMATION OF THE UNITED NATIONS

The idea of an international organization to oversee world affairs and prevent conflicts among and between nations was not something new. The League of Nations, the predecessor of the United Nations, had been established in 1919 after the end of World War I (1914–1918) with the express purpose of preventing another such war. In this role and many others, it failed. The aggression of Nazi Germany, Italy, and Imperial Japan against their neighbors in the interwar period signaled the end of the League of Nations. Although the league had been a flawed body, too weak to be able to resolve conflicts, it was clear by the end of World War II that there was still a need for a strong global organization to oversee international affairs—and to prevent another horrific world war.

Children with members of the Red Cross in Auschwitz, Poland, circa 1945. The horrific system of concentration camps established by the Nazis to systematically kill European Jews and other groups deemed "undesirable" was a main reason why the world community felt it necessary to draft a human rights declaration.

The total number of casualties—soldiers and civilians—in World War I is estimated at 37 million people. Approximately 70 million people died during the six years of World War II. Although fighting across the globe was savage and systematic bombing of cities was widespread in World War II, some of the most horrific deaths occurred in the concentration camps established by the Nazis across the territory they conquered in Europe. Anti-Semitism had been a basis of the Nazi platform since Hitler had risen to power in Germany in 1933.

The hatred of Jews and other "undesirable" groups, such as the Roma (commonly known as gypsies), homosexuals, Soviet prisoners of war, Catholics, and the mentally disabled, led to the Holocaust, a term that means "completely burned." While an estimated 6 million Jews were killed during the Holocaust, the total number of all groups killed by the Nazis could be as high as 11 million.

The discovery of the camps where Jews and others were held was a horrific experience for the Allied powers of Great Britain, the Soviet Union, and the United States, which liberated these camps. Jews and others deemed unfit by the Nazis for civil society were forcibly placed in the concentration camps and used for slave labor until they died of starvation, disease, fatigue, or other reasons. Others were placed in extermination camps, where they were systematically murdered, most usually through the use of gas chambers. The international community vowed that the nations of the world would never again allow such an atrocity to take place. However, the only way to ensure this would be to cooperate on an international scale as never before.

This was also an era in which liberal sentiment began to emerge more strongly than ever before in the United States and other nations—a political philosophy that broadly considers individual rights and liberties to be of the greatest importance. In *Casting Her Own Shadow: Eleanor Roosevelt and the Shaping of Postwar Liberalism*, Allida M. Black writes, "Stunned by the Holocaust and the rise of totalitarianism, liberals struggled to balance their commitment to a more humane world against their own awareness of the darkness of the human spirit."[1]

The term "United Nations" was first used by Franklin Delano Roosevelt as a way to refer to the Allied nations that were engaged in war against the Axis powers of Germany, Japan, and Italy. The nations, including China, Great Britain, the United States, and the Soviet Union, as well as many others, signed the Declaration by United Nations on January 1, 1942,

(continues on page 20)

THE IMPACT OF WORLD WAR II

In writing about the show of solidarity between nations to create an international agreement on human rights, Robert G. Patman describes the "unprecedented levels of human brutality" that people witnessed during World War II. The war, unlike previous wars, he says, "was distinctive in the sheer scale of human suffering which it caused."*

Overall, the war fought between the Allied and Axis powers resulted in the deaths of approximately 70 million people, many of them civilians. The most severe and shocking example of human brutality was the Holocaust, in which millions of people were systematically murdered by the Nazi regime, led by Adolf Hitler. During the rise of the Nazism, Jews in Germany had been increasingly singled out and suffered discrimination; as Germany conquered nearby nations, Jews (as well as other ethnic minorities) across Eastern Europe, Russia, and France were rounded up and sent to camps, where they were either worked to death or killed upon arrival.

Other examples of atrocities during World War II include the plight of the Russians after Germany's invasion. Hitler had previously signed a mutual nonaggression treaty with Joseph Stalin, but the German leader broke the pact when Nazi forces crossed the Russian border in June 1941. The German aggression left the Russians scrambling to defend themselves at first, and the Nazis committed atrocities against the many innocent civilians they encountered. In the small village of Khatyn, in Belarus, the German forces arrived on March 22, 1943; they gathered the 149 inhabitants of the village, half of which were children, into a barn and set it on fire, burning everyone inside alive. They then burned down every single house and building in the rest of the village. The Khatyn massacre was one of many;

Warsaw, Poland in ruins in 1945. Most of the major cities in Europe and Japan were leveled, in addition to large parts of Asia, the Pacific, and North Africa suffering catastrophic damage.

hundreds of other Belarusian villages were similarly wiped out in this manner. Over 2 million Belarusians perished in the war. (This massacre should not be confused with the 1940 Katyn massacre, in which thousands of Polish military officers, intellectuals, and civilian prisoners of war were executed by Soviet forces.)

On July 10, 1944, the German army attacked the village of Distomo in Greece. Rebels had attacked the invading Germans from the village, and the Germans took their revenge against the villagers in a horrific way. Two-hundred-eighteen villagers died, including women and children, as the Nazis went from house to house, brutalizing, raping, and killing the inhabitants. They also beheaded the village priest.

(continues)

(continued)

The American decision to drop atomic bombs on the Japanese cities of Nagasaki and Hiroshima in August 1945 remains a hotly debated issue. Although the action—the first and only time that a nuclear attack has ever been carried out—decisively ended the conflict, the toll in human lives was tremendous. In Hiroshima, the bomb killed approximately half the city's population, or 140,000 people; the Nagasaki bomb killed approximately 80,000. These figures do not reflect the people who later died from exposure to the high levels of radiation from the bomb's effects.

* Robert G. Patman, ed. *Universal Human Rights?* New York: St. Martin's Press, 2000, p. 1.

(continued from page 17)
recognizing that "complete victory over their enemies is essential to defend life, liberty, independence and religious freedom, and to preserve human rights and justice in their own lands as well as in other lands, and that they are now engaged in a common struggle against savage and brutal forces seeking to subjugate the world."[2] These nations pledged to use their full military and economic resources to fight the Axis powers.

This Declaration by United Nations later became the basis for the establishment of the organization of the same name. On April 25, 1945, the first meeting of the fledgling world body was hosted by the United States in the city of San Francisco, California. Although Italy had surrendered in 1943 and Germany would surrender in early May, the war was still being waged against Japan, which would not surrender until August 14, only after the United States dropped atomic bombs on the Japanese cities of Hiroshima and Nagasaki.

Officially known as the United Nations Conference on International Organization, it was attended by the representatives of 50 nations and of several nongovernmental organizations. During the conference, the nations drafted the United Nations Charter, which was ratified and signed by the members, leading to the official establishment of the United Nations in October 1945.

Article 1 of the charter lays out the four main purposes of the United Nations:

1. To maintain international peace and security, and to that end: to take effective collective measures for the prevention and removal of threats to the peace, and for the suppression of acts of aggression or other breaches of the peace, and to bring about by peaceful means, and in conformity with the principles of justice and international law, adjustment or settlement of international disputes or situations which might lead to a breach of the peace;
2. To develop friendly relations among nations based on respect for the principle of equal rights and self-determination of peoples, and to take other appropriate measures to strengthen universal peace;
3. To achieve international co-operation in solving international problems of an economic, social, cultural, or humanitarian character, and in promoting and encouraging respect for human rights and for fundamental freedoms for all without distinction as to race, sex, language, or religion; and
4. To be a centre for harmonizing the actions of nations in the attainment of these common ends.[3]

The General Assembly is the main legislative body of the United Nations, to which all member nations have a representative and in which all member nations can raise issues or

A view of the first organizational meeting of the United Nations, held in San Francisco, California, from April 25 to June 26, 1945. This convention resulted in the creation of the United Nations Charter.

concerns. The Security Council, made up of a select group of nations, has authoritative power to make binding decisions by which all member nations must abide. Unlike its predecessor, the League of Nations, the United Nations has an armed force, though it is not a military force. Rather, the peacekeeping force, nicknamed the "Blue Berets" for their distinctive headgear, are sent to areas of conflict to maintain peace; the members of this force are sent voluntarily by member nations.

The formation of the United Nations in 1945 signaled a major shift in world politics and international relations. It meant that nations had agreed that certain principles were universal and that diplomacy was the key to avoiding another major global conflict such as the one that had transpired between 1939 and 1945.

THE QUESTION OF HUMAN RIGHTS

One of the first tasks that the fledgling United Nations concerned itself with was the question of human rights, a subject President Roosevelt had addressed in a speech several years earlier. On January 6, 1941—as war was raging in Europe and Asia, but before the United States was involved—the president addressed Congress about the war and American security. He began by emphasizing that "at no previous time has American security been as seriously threatened from without as it is today." He also outlined what he called the "four freedoms," which every nation on earth should strive to provide its citizens:

> The first is freedom of speech and expression—everywhere in the world.
> The second is freedom of every person to worship God in his own way—everywhere in the world.
> The third is freedom from want, which, translated into world terms, means economic understandings which will secure to every nation a healthy peacetime life for its inhabitants—everywhere in the world.
> The fourth is freedom from fear, which, translated into world terms, means a world-wide reduction of armaments to such a point and in such a thorough fashion that no nation will be in a position to commit an act of physical aggression against any neighbor—anywhere in the world.[4]

Years later, this much-admired speech would help shape the work of the committee of the Universal Declaration of Human Rights, chaired by Roosevelt's widow. The former president's emphasis on individual human liberties was an important one, especially because he added that these freedoms should be enjoyed by people all over the world, no matter their ethnicity, race, religion, or national citizenship.

And yet, the discussion of human rights is hardly simple. There are several issues of ideology that affect the main subject. For example, who grants human rights? Are they given to people, or are they innate? Who deserves to benefit from human rights? Are human rights universal, or does one have to be a citizen of a particular nation to benefit from and claim these rights?

More specifically, are human rights a matter of contract between the government and the people (such as in the case of the Magna Carta, the charter signed in 1215 between England's monarch and his people)? Are they a matter of natural law? Natural law tradition, according to Chris Brown, "holds that human beings have an essential nature which dictates that certain kinds of human goods are always and everywhere desired as necessary for human flourishing; because of this essential nature we can think of there being common moral standards that govern all human relations."[5] In other words, human rights are not of a legal nature, but of a moral nature; the enforcement of human rights is needed and should be universal so that the human race can continue to advance and flourish.

A major issue that would face the UN Commission on Human Rights would be whether or not the rights of the individual take priority over the rights of the general population, or the "common good." (This would be an especially important issue for the Soviet Union and other states with Communist governments.) Would it even be possible for the global community—comprising so many different ethnicities, cultures, races, and religions—to agree on a single course of action for ensuring human rights?

Finally, and perhaps most importantly: What would be the UN's specific role in relation to human rights? Should it produce a simple list of rights to which all human beings are theoretically entitled? Or should it produce a covenant, or a convention—a more legally binding document to which all signatories must adhere?

These questions and more would have to be discussed and settled if the Human Rights Commission were to succeed in producing a document. But that was not where the task ended: After the document's production, it would have to be approved by the UN in order to have any meaning.

To draft a statement on human rights that would be approved by the full UN General Assembly was daunting and needed careful leadership. As Mary Ann Glendon, author of *A World Made New: Eleanor Roosevelt and the Universal Declaration of Human Rights*, explains:

> The draft would first have to be approved by the full Commission on Human Rights, then circulated to all member states for comments. Those comments would undoubtedly require revisions by the drafting committee. The revised document would be returned to the full Committee for final consideration. The Commission would then submit its draft for review by the Economic and Social Council, which would decide whether or not to recommend it to the General Assembly, where it would have to undergo preliminary scrutiny by the Third Committee on Social, Humanitarian, and Cultural Affairs.[6]

Only then would the statement on human rights go to a full review and vote before the UN General Assembly, scheduled for the fall of 1948. The task indeed seemed overwhelming, but it would find a true, careful, and pragmatic leader in Eleanor Roosevelt.

The Development of a Leader

THE "GRANNY"

A famous cartoon that appeared in the *Washington Post* perfectly captured the widespread fame Eleanor Roosevelt achieved as first lady: it depicts a little immigrant boy and his mother aboard a ship coming to Ellis Island. As he spies the Statue of Liberty, the boy says, "Of course I know who that is. It's Mrs. Roosevelt."[1]

Anna Eleanor Roosevelt was born on October 11, 1884, into the prominent Roosevelt family of New York. Her uncle Theodore—who would serve as president from 1901 to 1909—was her godfather and always referred to her as his favorite niece. Her father, Elliot, Theodore's younger brother, lacked his brother's resilience and work ethic—in fact, Elliot spent much of his time gambling and drinking, which caused his wife and family much distress. Lois Scharf writes: "The polo games, the hunts, the horse shows, the exclusive clubs—all were not merely sampled with restraint but relished with insatiable appetite. He played games with an energy that bordered on recklessness."[2]

Eleanor's mother, Anna, after whom she was named, was a woman renowned in society for her beauty. Having such a lovely mother, however, was not helpful to young Eleanor. As she grew older, she became aware of the fact that she did not meet her mother's expectations in terms of looks and social graces. "For her daughter to grow up and excel in activities that had come to mean so much to her," writes Scharf, "to make a striking debut and win the admiration of countless beaux, the child must be beautiful and sparkling. Apparently from birth, the younger Anna Eleanor was neither."[3]

As a child, Eleanor had a somber, serious demeanor. Her mother took to calling her "granny" as a way to highlight how much older she seemed. The nickname stuck, and it caused Eleanor much sorrow and embarrassment. As Scharf writes, "'Granny' both created and described the awkwardness and unhappiness that clung to the child."[4] In fact, Eleanor was actually a good-looking girl, with attractive blue eyes and soft brown hair. Despite this, her mother would focus on other features, such as Eleanor's large teeth, which protruded awkwardly, causing the child to focus on her shortcomings rather than her advantages.

When Eleanor was 8, her 29-year-old, vivacious mother died of diphtheria following a surgery. Her father died two years later, in 1894, due to binge drinking brought on by chronic alcoholism. Eleanor's maternal grandmother, a loving and caring woman who was also strict and demanding, raised her and her younger brother, Hall. Her world was one of odd contrasts; she and Hall lived in her grandmother's austere household, but they still participated in the Roosevelt clan's events, such as balls and dances. Eleanor never was able to fit into this glamorous world very well, mostly because she did not possess the bubbly, charming personality of other girls her age.

She did well in her studies, however, perhaps retreating into the world of books and learning as a solace to her loneliness. At 15, she was sent to Allenswood, a finishing school near London, England. The intellectual atmosphere at Allenswood was stimulating for an already insightful girl. While there, she deeply enjoyed long discussions of literature and philosophy and also traveled throughout Europe. During her time in Europe, her uncle Theodore became president of the United States, lending Eleanor a new prestige.

When she returned to New York at age 18, she fell back into a state of sadness and depression. She and her brother were being shuttled between different family members, causing Eleanor to tell her aunt, "I have no real home."[5]

BUDDING SOCIAL ACTIVIST

In the early 1900s, many young women in elite New York circles had begun to involve themselves—however superficially—in social causes. Eleanor, like many other young women of her age and status, joined the Junior League, a club for girls to practice their charitable skills. At the time, many immigrants coming into New York City were met with low-wage jobs and poor housing conditions. Poverty tainted many sections of the city and many of the city's elite donated their time and money to help.

Eleanor became involved, through the Junior League, with the Rivington Settlement House in Manhattan. Rivington was modeled after one of the first social service agencies in the country, Hull House, which had been founded by social activist Jane Addams in Chicago, Illinois, in the late 1800s. Like Hull House, Rivington provided not just social relief, but also job training, literacy classes, and other services to help poor people improve their lives and the futures of their families.

At Rivington Settlement House, Eleanor gave dancing lessons to the daughters of Jewish and Italian immigrants. Scharf notes that these girls enjoyed the distraction from the difficulty of their everyday lives and that "they adored their teacher, who treated them with genuine kindness and who taught her classes with total commitment and personal satisfaction."[6] Excited by her work and enlightened by the conditions she saw people living in, Eleanor also enrolled in the New York Consumers' League, where she focused on improving the lives of lower-class women. She toured some of the factories and industries where these women worked to learn about their low pay and working conditions.

Despite having been moved by what she saw, Eleanor belonged to a different class of New Yorkers, and she could not get as involved as she may have wanted. While charity work was considered a good thing for a New York debutante to have on her social "résumé," especially for the niece of the American president, it was not expected—and indeed, would not be approved of—for her to interact with the lower classes or be involved in their world in any meaningful way.

FRANKLIN DELANO ROOSEVELT

Franklin Delano Roosevelt was Eleanor's distant relation, a fifth cousin, and she had previously met him at social events and balls held by the Roosevelts. The two fell in love, but were persuaded by his mother to keep their love a secret for one year as a test of their devotion to each other. This also meant that they had to be chaperoned whenever they were together, since they were not formally engaged, but the 19-year-old Eleanor and the 20-year-old Franklin wrote long letters to each other and managed to survive that year with their feelings still intact.

When they married on March 17, 1905, President Theodore Roosevelt gave the bride away. It was a celebrity-studded affair, with some of the nation's most prestigious and well-known people present. The couple then settled down to making a life together. Franklin was finishing his studies at Columbia Law School, and Eleanor focused on becoming the dedicated wife she was expected to be. In early 1906, they had their first child, a daughter, Anna Eleanor, and Eleanor Roosevelt focused on the demands of new motherhood.

Franklin Roosevelt was an ambitious young man who looked at Theodore Roosevelt as a role model. While he loved Eleanor, finding comfort and strength in her serious, steady demeanor, he also was pleased to have married the president's favorite niece. Like Theodore, Franklin quickly became involved in politics, running for a seat in the New York legislature in 1910. When he won, Eleanor quickly merged the roles of mother and wife with that of a politician's spouse, hosting parties and teas and attending political rallies and events.

By 1916, the Roosevelts had six children, although one, a boy, died as an infant. In 1917, when the United States entered World War I, Eleanor volunteered with the American Red Cross and spent time working in navy hospitals with wounded servicemen. Later, she joined the League of Women Voters, the Women's Trade Union League, and the Democratic Party—her husband's political party—after women were given the right to vote in 1920. In 1921, Franklin was afflicted with polio, which would leave him in a wheelchair for the rest of his life. For a time, he thought his political career was finished. With Eleanor's support, however, he became governor of New York State in 1928.

AN OUTSPOKEN FIRST LADY

In November 1932, FDR was elected president of the United States and immediately faced the crisis of the Great Depression— the severe economic downturn that began with the stock market crash in 1929 and did not end until the beginning of World War II. FDR's skill in handling the crisis—his New Deal programs are largely credited with regulating the business world, creating jobs, and keeping many Americans from starvation—made him so popular that he was elected to four terms in office, more than any other president before or since.

Eleanor Roosevelt is photographed on a coal train about to enter the Willow Grow Mine in Bellaire, Ohio, on May 22, 1935. The activist first lady went there to gain firsthand information concerning mine conditions.

When war broke out in Europe in 1939, following Germany's invasion of Poland on September 1, FDR tried to keep the United States out of the war, but sold arms and supplies to the Allies, primarily Great Britain and France. When Japanese forces attacked the American naval base at Pearl Harbor in Hawaii on December 7, 1941, however, the United States entered the war against the Axis powers and helped turn the tide in favor of the Allies.

During the war, Eleanor was invaluable as first lady, showing her activism and political intuition to the advantage of the

(continues on page 35)

ELEANOR ROOSEVELT'S SENSE OF JUSTICE

The Civil War, which had abolished slavery in all territories and regions of the United States, had ended in 1865, but African Americans did not enjoy full equal rights during Franklin Roosevelt's presidency. A series of segregationist laws, referred to as Jim Crow laws after a popular, racist character of the same name, essentially separated American society into black and white. Black Americans were limited in terms of where they could live, where they could attend school, and even from which water fountains they could drink and which seats they could take on public buses.

Eleanor Roosevelt had always considered segregation to be unjust. As first lady, many of her actions were limited by the White House policies, and Franklin Roosevelt did not want to take aggressive actions to correct racism and discrimination in the midst of economic crisis and war. However, there were several moments in which his wife did take action, thus cementing her reputation as the moral backbone of the administration.

One example of Eleanor Roosevelt's moves to combat racism concerned Marian Anderson, a popular African-American singer. Born in Philadelphia in 1897, she suffered racial discrimination all her life, including being turned away from an all-white music school because she was black. Despite such adversity, she persevered in her dream of becoming a singer. Her talent shone, and she joined the New York Philharmonic in 1925, instantly becoming a success. She toured throughout the United States and Europe and was critically acclaimed for her contralto voice.

Racism continued to plague her, however. In a famous incident in 1939, Anderson's manager tried to schedule a

Pictured, First Lady Eleanor Roosevelt and Marian Anderson, one of the most celebrated singers of the twentieth century.

concert for her to sing before an integrated audience at Constitution Hall in Washington, D.C. She was prevented from doing so by the Daughters of the American Revolution (DAR), an organization of women who can trace their lineage back to the nation's Founding Fathers and the generation of Americans who helped achieve independence from

(continues)

(continued)

Great Britain. Many prominent and distinguished American women have been members, including Eleanor Roosevelt. Because Constitution Hall had been built by the DAR's fund-raising efforts, the group was able to control who appeared there. They had a policy that did not allow black and white attendees to mix in the same hall, in accordance with the segregation policy of the day.

Many of the DAR's members were outraged by the organization's obstruction of Anderson's performance. Alternate venues for her to perform met with little success until the first lady stepped in and took action. Roosevelt wrote a letter to the president of the DAR, in which she resigned her membership: "I am in complete disagreement with the attitude taken in refusing Constitution Hall to a great artist. You have set an example which seems to be unfortunate, and I feel obliged to send in to you my resignation. You had an opportunity to lead in an enlightened way, and it seems to me that your organization has failed."*

Furthermore, Roosevelt arranged for Anderson to sing in an open-air concert, free for all attendees, on the steps of the Lincoln Memorial—a fitting backdrop because Abraham Lincoln was the president who issued the Emancipation Proclamation, the document ending slavery. Held on Easter Sunday in 1939, the concert attracted 75,000 attendees and was aired on the radio, featuring Anderson's rendition of "My Country, 'Tis of Thee." After her performance, Anderson was a guest at the White House. In July 1939, the first lady presented her with the Spingarn Medal of the National Association for the Advancement of Colored People.

---

* "Eleanor Roosevelt Letter." National Archives. http://www.archives.gov/exhibits/american_originals/eleanor.html.

(continued from page 31)
Americans. She visited the troops abroad to raise their morale and also served as an informal diplomat to the other Allied governments. Because of her husband's health problems, she often delivered speeches in his stead or sat in on meetings and then reported to him, often lending him sound advice that he followed. She also disagreed with her husband and his administration's policies on many occasions, but FDR had learned to expect this of his intelligent wife and accepted her criticism in the genuine, helpful way it was intended.

For example, she was a firm believer in civil rights for African Americans, despite the fact that many members of her own Democratic Party, most notably Southern politicians, supported segregationist policies. Nevertheless, Eleanor felt that all Americans were entitled to equal rights and was appalled by the treatment of blacks in the South as well as in many parts of the North.

Roosevelt was also an advocate of women's rights and saw clearly that women needed to be more involved in American political life. This stand, however, represented a major evolution in her political perspective. It is important to remember that Roosevelt was born in 1884, during the Victorian era, when women were expected to be homemakers and devoted wives. They were not expected to proffer opinions or to hold intellectual conversations; indeed, had Eleanor not been married to a politician with a progressive bent, she may never have immersed herself in the important issues of the day or formed her own progressive opinions. During her husband's early political career, she had been too busy raising five children and supervising her household to learn much about politics beyond what she saw her husband doing. She said once about the debate regarding the right of women to vote, "I considered any stand at that time was outside my field of work . . . I was too much taken with the family to give it much thought."[7]

Eleanor Roosevelt possessed an open mind and an intellectual curiosity. She was not stubborn and could change her views based on increased knowledge, and she often did. By the time of her husband's death in April 1945, she had made her mark as "first lady of the world" because of her championing of the rights of women, the poor, minorities, refugees, and other people afflicted by circumstances beyond their control. Her work on her husband's behalf during his administration had also honed her skills at compromise, working effectively toward a goal, and administrative duties. She had made herself a highly effective and invaluable advisor and aide during his presidency.

Allida M. Black notes that Eleanor Roosevelt's "political career did not end when her husband died."[8] In fact, she continued her dedication to social causes as before. In January 1947, shortly before the first meeting of the Human Rights Commission, Roosevelt was named "the woman most admired by other American women."[9] Her popularity around the world, especially after the debate with Soviet delegate Andrey Vyshinsky in the United Nations, was quite high.

Indeed, she would prove to be the perfect advocate—the perfect leader—to tackle the task of the draft on human rights.

The Team

THE EVER-EXPANDING COMMISSION

The year 1947 began in earnest for Eleanor Roosevelt as the project to write an international bill of human rights got underway. In drafting the groundbreaking statement on universal human rights, Roosevelt had the benefit of working with a team of important, diverse colleagues from all over the world.

The full Human Rights Commission was a large group consisting of 18 members. This group's first meeting was held at Lake Success, New York, between January 27 and February 10, 1947. Their first task was to select a chairperson, who to no one's surprise was Roosevelt, by then a well-known champion of human rights and humanitarian causes.

The members of the Human Rights Commission quickly realized that they could not draft a statement on human rights in such a large group. Thus, according to Mary Ann Glendon, the commission "unanimously approved a . . . resolution that a 'preliminary draft' of an international bill of rights should be prepared for submission at the Commission's second session by the three officers of the Commission,"[1] with the help of the UN Secretariat on Human Rights, whose leader was John Humphrey, a Canadian legal scholar. The drafting subcommittee included Roosevelt, Chinese representative Peng-Chun (P.C.) Chang, and Lebanese representative Charles Malik.

At their first meeting, the three officers of the subcommittee decided that John Humphrey, because of his access to resources regarding other documents of a similar nature and the ability of his office and staff to provide research, would prepare the draft, which would then be reviewed by the subcommittee before it was presented to the larger committee. Humphrey—the author of several well-regarded papers and articles on international law—gladly took on the task, but he was advised by the others to "avoid an excessively Western orientation"[2] and to carefully reference other documents. Glendon notes, "The decision to entrust the first draft to Humphrey made good sense."[3]

The makeup of this subcommittee would soon prove controversial, however, because the French and the Soviets objected to such a small group being involved in the preparation of the draft. Where were the European and the Russian voices? In response to their concern, Roosevelt agreed to expand the drafting subcommittee to include members from Australia, Chile, France, Great Britain, and the Soviet Union.

At the first meeting of the now-expanded subcommittee to draft the declaration, held on June 9, 1947, eight people in addition to Roosevelt—Charles Malik of Lebanon, René Cassin of France, P.C. Chang of China, John Humphrey of Canada, William Hodgson of Australia, Geoffrey Wilson of Great

Eleanor Roosevelt, chair of the UN Committee on Human Rights, holds a headphone to her ear during a June 1947 meeting of the drafting committee.

Britain, Hernán Santa Cruz of Chile, and Vladimir Koretsky of the Soviet Union—sat around the table, eager to begin their work, and yet wondering how to proceed or even how to approach the broad, and vague, issue of human rights. Each brought a unique perspective to the work at hand, perspectives that would often clash during the drafting process.

CHARLES MALIK

As they began the task of drafting the declaration, Lebanese member Charles Habib Malik admitted that he and the others felt "completely lost; we had no conception of how to proceed with the task entrusted to us."[4] One of Roosevelt's strongest advocates and most hardworking colleagues on the committee, Malik had been selected rapporteur (or secretary) of the commission at its initial meeting. A tall man with unruly and curly dark hair, large, dark eyes, and a large, beaked nose, he made quite a striking figure around the United Nations and was known not just for his looks but for his intellectual manner and disposition. Malik believed deeply in the value of the committee's task, and he wanted it to succeed.

The son of Arab parents, Malik was born in northern Lebanon in 1906 and raised in the Greek Orthodox faith. As his father was a doctor, the young Malik enjoyed an excellent elementary and middle school education at the local Christian schools. He later attended the prestigious American University of Beirut, where he studied mathematics and physics. After developing an interest in philosophy, he lived and studied in Germany for some time, but left because of the oppressive political climate of the 1930s—the age of the rise of Nazism and Hitler. On one occasion, street thugs beat him because of his Semitic looks; at that point, he knew he had to leave. He completed his doctorate in philosophy at Harvard University in the United States, then returned to the American University in Beirut, where he established the university's philosophy department and guided its growth and development.

Despite being an academic, Malik was drawn to politics. In 1945, he served as Lebanon's ambassador to the United States. One of his first assignments was to represent Lebanon at the inaugural conference of the United Nations in San Francisco that same year.

As a member of the human rights subcommittee, he advocated the natural law theory of human rights. He worried that

A 1953 photo of Charles Malik, the former head of American University at Beirut's philosophy department, who served as the Lebanese minister to the United Nations and on the UN Commission on Human Rights.

the emphasis of many people on economic needs and rights—the need to work, eat, have safe housing, and the like—stressed the animal needs of mankind, rather than the things that set people apart from animals, such as the ability to reason, express oneself, voice one's political thoughts, and others. In 1948, Malik wrote that he feared that "human rights" would be erroneously defined by economic rather than intellectual needs: "Unless man's proper nature, unless his mind and spirit are brought out, set apart, protected, and promoted, the struggle for human rights is a sham and a mockery."[5] In joining the committee, Malik wanted to make sure that the final declaration would be binding upon nations, rather than simply a statement or definition of human rights.

RENÉ CASSIN

Because he had witnessed the devastation wrought by two world wars in his homeland of France, few members of the committee to draft the Declaration of Human Rights had more acute insight into the issue of human rights than René Cassin.

Born into a Jewish family in Bayonne in 1887, René Cassin was the son of a merchant. Like his colleague Charles Malik, Cassin had excelled in academics as a young boy. He received his early education in Nice, France, and later attended the University of Aix-en-Provence, where he received a dual degree in the humanities and law in 1908. Upon graduation, he embarked upon a legal career, working at the Court of Paris. In 1914, he completed a doctoral degree in juridical, economic, and political sciences, but he was soon called to serve in the French military during World War I. In 1916, he was injured in battle by shrapnel and was saved only by the fact that his mother, who worked as a nurse, insisted that he undergo surgery. The injury caused him to use a cane for the rest of his life.

After being discharged from the military, Cassin began a career as a professor of law at Aix-en-Provence. He also became heavily involved in helping France recover from the war. In 1918, he established the French Federation of Disabled War Veterans and served as its president for many years. He also accepted a post as vice president of the High Council for Wards of the Nation, to help children who had been orphaned because of the war. He then served as French ambassador to the League of Nations from 1924 to 1938, which gave him valuable parliamentary experience.

After France was occupied by Germany during World War II, Cassin became a legal advisor to Charles de Gaulle, the leader of the Free French Forces and an important member of France's government-in-exile. Cassin not only advised de Gaulle, but also worked diligently to preserve his country's educational institutions, serving as the National Commissioner of Justice and Public Instruction from 1941 to 1943 and on the Permanent Conference of Allied Ministers of Education from 1942 until 1945. From 1943 to 1945, Cassin served on the United Nations Commission on Inquiry into War Crimes.

During the French occupation, the Germans issued a death sentence for Cassin. (The Nazi police placed a black seal on his apartment door in Paris, which he kept there long after the war ended.) While Cassin escaped personal injury, his extended family did not: During the war, 29 of Cassin's relatives, including his sister, perished in Nazi concentration camps.

His vast expertise on the legal, philosophical, and political aspects of human rights made him invaluable to the committee. In fact, Roosevelt would grow to rely on him as one of the most active contributors to the writing of the draft that would go for approval before the General Assembly.

PENG-CHUN CHANG

Peng-Chun (or P.C.) Chang, the representative from China, was an important asset to the committee for two reasons: He was a creative negotiator who helped resolve many disputes, and he brought an Eastern perspective on human rights and issues to the committee that helped ensure that the draft declaration was universal.

A former professor at Nankai University in Beijing, Chang was selected as the committee's vice chair. Born in China in 1893, he received a scholarship from the U.S. government to study in America. In 1921, after completing his Ph.D. in the field of Chinese studies at Columbia University in New York City, he returned to China to teach. As his talents lay in many areas, Chang was something of a renaissance man; he was also a noted playwright, poet, and literary critic.

After the Japanese invasion of China in 1937, Chang joined the resistance movement but was forced to flee for his life.

HIGH COMMISSIONER FOR HUMAN RIGHTS

One of the most significant advances made by the United Nations, after the signing of the Universal Declaration of Human Rights, was the establishment of the office of High Commissioner for Human Rights. This permanent position oversees the UN's work around the world related to the protection of human rights.

One of the most influential people to serve as high commissioner was Mary Robinson, who was appointed in 1997 at a time when the UN had merged the offices of the commissioner with its Centre for Human Rights. A former law professor, Robinson had previously served as president of Ireland for seven years. Ireland's long history of oppression and turmoil helped make her familiar with human rights issues. During her presidency, she was also active in the field of international human rights and visited the

Following Japan's defeat in World War II, the Chinese government used his communication skills toward a diplomatic end. He was tasked with helping the Western countries understand the Japanese atrocities committed in China, especially during what is now known as the "rape of Nanking," a six-week period in which thousands of women and girls were raped and hundreds of thousands of civilians were murdered in that city by Japanese soldiers. He later served as the Chinese ambassador to Turkey and Chile.

Chang was greatly influenced by the teachings of Confucius, the great Chinese philosopher, and he often brought those lessons to bear on the work of the committee as a way of resolving disputes. Because he had a deep understanding of

African nation of Rwanda in 1994 after more than a million people were massacred there. Robinson received the CARE Humanitarian Award for her efforts on behalf of the African nation of Somalia during its crisis.

As of 2009, the high commissioner is Navanethem Pillay, who hails from South Africa. Born in the region of Natal, she is active in women's causes and has worked with the Women's National Coalition and also helped establish Equality Now, an international women's organization. After earning her law degree from Harvard University, she worked for many years to help defend South Africans who advocated an end to apartheid rule. She also taught, as well as worked in administration, at the university level. After the apartheid system was dismantled in the early 1990s, she was appointed to serve on the nation's High Court. She also worked with the United Nations for eight years as a judge on the criminal tribunal for the Rwandan genocide, prior to being named to the position of High Commissioner for Human Rights.

both Eastern and Western philosophy, for example, he was able to show opponents on an issue that they actually shared common ground.

JOHN HUMPHREY

Canadian John Peters Humphrey was born in Hampton, New Brunswick, in 1905. His early childhood was filled with tremendous personal obstacles: At the age of six, he lost his left arm in an accident; when he was 11, he was orphaned. Though he struggled to make a life for himself during long years at a boys' boarding school, he excelled academically. After attaining his law degree, he practiced law until 1936 before turning to a career in teaching. He quickly earned a reputation as an expert in international law.

When World War II broke out, he was prevented from serving in the military due to his disability, but as Glendon notes, "though he had been unable to fight in the war, he could perhaps help to shape the peace."[6] His chance to do so came when he was asked to serve as the head of the UN Secretariat's Division of Human Rights in 1946. At the time of his appointment, he was a professor of law at McGill University, but he would later complete a 20-year career at the United Nations. He returned to teaching in 1966 and worked for human rights in Canada, where he helped found the Canadian Human Rights Foundation and the Canadian branch of Amnesty International.

SANTA CRUZ, WILSON, AND KORETSKY

History has paid less attention to the contributions of Santa Cruz, Wilson, and Koretsky. Alexei Pavlov, one of several representatives sent by the Soviet Union to the Human Rights Commission, soon replaced Koretsky. Wilson, of Great Britain, had replaced Charles Dukes (Lord Dukeston) and sought to encourage the committee to work on a binding covenant rather than a statement of rights (in fact, the British foreign office had instructed him to work toward this end). Santa

Cruz—a professor, military instructor, and judge in Chile who served on Chile's Superior Military Court—came to the proceedings with one primary goal: to ensure that socioeconomic rights were regarded with as much importance as civil and political rights.

The Drafting Process

THE SECRETARIAT'S OUTLINE

According to the committee's charge, John Humphrey and his staff prepared an initial draft of the declaration. Mary Ann Glendon writes, "Aiming for comprehensiveness, John Humphrey had instructed his staff at the UN to study all the world's existing constitutions and rights instruments, as well as the suggestions that had poured in to the Secretariat from members of the Commission, outside organizations, and even from various interested individuals."[1] Humphrey's draft was exhaustive: He provided a list of 48 individual items that covered the gamut of all rights that had previously been addressed by governments and organizations around the world, including "the right to life," "the right to personal liberty," "the right to resist oppression and tyranny," "the right to education," "the right to own personal property," "the right to a fair share of rest and leisure," and even "the right and duty to perform socially useful work."[2]

Each article was followed by a detailed annotation and an explanation of the article's relevance to the committee's work. The draft totaled 400 pages in length, confirming the UN's later assessment that the secretariat had put together "the most exhaustive documentation on the subject of human rights ever assembled."[3]

PREVIOUS MODELS

The Secretariat's outline, also known as the Humphrey draft, relied heavily on previous models such as the English Magna Carta, the U.S. Declaration of Independence and Bill of Rights, and the French Declaration of the Rights of Man and of the Citizen.

The Magna Carta—a contract between an English king and his subjects—is a Latin term meaning "great charter." In 1215, a group of English barons rebelled against King John; in order to stall their actions, the unpopular monarch agreed to sign a contract explicitly outlining his people's rights. Although King John used the Magna Carta as a way to maintain his throne for a short time until he could regain the upper hand in his struggle with the nobility, the contents of the charter would prove to be vitally important to future common and constitutional law. For the first time, an English king recognized the rights of his people (in this case noblemen, not common people) in writing. For example, the charter ensured that subjects would not have their property unlawfully seized, as in Article 31: "Neither we nor our bailiffs will take some one else's wood for [repairing] castles or for doing any other work of ours, except by the will of him to whom the wood belongs."[4] It also protected the safe passage of people in and out of the country, as in Article 42:

> It shall be lawful in future for any one (excepting always those imprisoned or outlawed in accordance with the law

of the kingdom, and natives of any country at war with us, and merchants, who shall be treated as is above provided) to leave our kingdom and to return, safe and secure by land and water, except for a short period in time of war, on grounds of public policy—reserving always the allegiance due to us.

It also clarified (however interestingly) the reasons for which one could be imprisoned, as in Article 54: "No one shall be arrested or imprisoned upon the appeal of a woman, for the death of any other than her husband."[5] While some of the rights outlined seem strange today, the Magna Carta amended the conditions the nobility had been suffering under at the hands of the monarchy. It also demonstrated that no one, including the sovereign, was above the law.

Documents forged during the American revolutionary period of the late eighteenth century also served as a model for the Human Rights Commission. The Declaration of Independence, written in 1776, contained very useful language, such as a set of "self-evident" truths, including "that all men are created equal; that they are endowed by their Creator with certain inalienable rights; that among these are life, liberty, and the pursuit of happiness." It also stated that the role of government is to protect and enforce these rights for individuals, and that governments "derived their just powers from the consent of the governed." The declaration is also illustrative in describing the abuses that had been perpetrated against Americans by the British monarch. Those abuses, which the signers believed infringed upon their innate human rights, included the following:

He [the king] has refused to pass other laws for the accommodation of large districts of people, unless those people would relinquish the right of representation in the legislature; a right inestimable to them and formidable to tyrants only. . . .

He has dissolved representative houses, repeatedly for opposing with manly firmness, his invasions on the rights of the people.[6]

The king was also charged with "quartering large bodies of armed troops among us; . . . For depriving us, in many cases, of the benefit of trial by jury; For transporting us beyond seas to be tried for pretended offenses"[7] and many other accusations.

This list of grievances describes how the rights of individuals have been withheld or violated; it does not outline a list of rights that should be upheld. By contrast, the Bill of Rights, the first 10 amendments added to the U.S. Constitution in 1791, does the latter: It sets forth the specific rights of U.S. citizens that must be upheld and enforced by their government. These include the rights outlined in the First Amendment: "Congress shall make no law respecting an establishment of religion, or prohibiting the free exercise thereof; or abridging the freedom of speech, or of the press; or the right of the people peaceably to assemble, and to petition the government for a redress of grievances." The Fourth Amendment states: "The right of the people to be secure . . . against unreasonable searches and seizures, shall not be violated, and no warrants shall issue, but upon probable cause, supported by oath or affirmation, and particularly describing the place to be searched, and the persons or things to be seized." The Fifth Amendment states:

> No person shall be held to answer for a capital, or otherwise infamous crime, unless on a presentment or indictment of a grand jury, except in cases arising in the land or naval forces, or in the militia, when in actual service in time of war or public danger; nor shall any person be subject for the same offense to be twice put in jeopardy of life or limb; nor shall be compelled in any criminal case to be a witness against himself, nor be deprived of life, liberty, or property, without due process of law; nor shall private property be taken for public use, without just compensation.[8]

The French Revolution, which overthrew the French monarchy in 1789, also led to the creation of a statement of

Eleanor Roosevelt holds a poster of the Universal Declaration of Human Rights at Lake Success, New York, in November 1949.

rights. Like the U.S. Declaration of Independence, the French Declaration of the Rights of Man and Citizen, adopted in August 1789, affirms that "men are born and remain free and equal in rights," and that the goal of a government is to preserve individual rights, which are listed specifically as "liberty, property, security, and resistance to oppression." Interestingly, it also delineated the limitations of rights by stating, "Liberty consists of the power to do whatever is not injurious to others; thus the enjoyment of the natural rights of every man has for its limits only those that assure other members of society the enjoyment of those same rights; such limits may be determined only by law." The declaration also stated expressly, "Free communication of ideas and opinions is one of the most precious of the rights of man."[9]

THE FORMULATION OF A STATEMENT

With the Humphrey draft and the previous models in hand, the commission resumed an earlier discussion to define their general purpose and goals. Eleanor Roosevelt, under the direction of the U.S. government, pushed for the committee to formulate a bill of human rights that would be universal and applicable to people all over the world. Others on the commission, including Hansa Mehta of India, wanted a document that would be more legally binding, such as a covenant.

Mehta, who belonged to a prestigious Brahman (the highest ranking in India's caste system) family, was born in 1897, when India was still a colony of Great Britain. Her family was liberal in its views and highly educated. Mehta was among the first Indian women to complete a college degree, and she later sailed to England to continue her studies in journalism. There, and later when she lived in the United States, she became involved in the women's movement.

When she returned to India, she married a man from another caste, which caused a controversy, though her immediate family supported the marriage. (Since ancient times, Indian society has been divided into thousands of subgroups, or castes, called *Jāti*.) In Bombay, she became active in education and social causes. In addition to her activist work and her work as a translator (translating Shakespeare and other Western writers into Gujarati, a language native to the Indian state of Gujarat), Mehta became parliamentary secretary to the minister of education and health. Soon she became active in the civil disobedience movement of Mahatma Gandhi, who used nonviolent methods to force the British to free India from imperial rule. Mehta was arrested and imprisoned by the British forces many times for her participation in demonstrations and other forms of protest. She also took over the helm of the women's movement in India, pushing for a Charter of Women's Rights. After independence from Britain became a reality in 1947, Mehta continued to be active in politics.

At the time of Mehta's appointment to the Human Rights Commission, however, India was still on the cusp of its struggle

René Cassin, the noted humanitarian and jurist, was recognized in his lifetime as one of the world's foremost proponents of human rights. In 1968, he was awarded the Nobel Peace Prize for his work on the draft of the Declaration of Human Rights that was approved by the UN General Assembly in 1948.

for liberation (the commission's first meeting took place in January 1947, and Indian independence would be realized later that year, in August). Perhaps her experiences led Mehta to insist that the document the commission produced have some "teeth," some method of enforcement to ensure that the nations that signed it would fulfill their obligations. Glendon writes that, along with the Australian representative, William Hodgson, Mehta was "adamant that an international bill of rights would be meaningless without some machinery for enforcement."[10] Suggested possibilities included an international tribunal to try war criminals, or again, a document that was more of a covenant than a simple declaration of rights. The British representative also favored such a route, to make the commission's work more meaningful. Others wondered if a document with teeth would interfere with a nation's sovereign rights. In the end, a compromise was reached to work on two different types of documents: a declaration of rights as well as a covenant.

The subcommittee charged with drafting the actual declaration was narrowed yet again, as it was suggested that eight people were too many. Now that the Humphrey draft was in hand, the subcommittee's size was cut in half, to include just Cassin, Malik, Wilson, and Roosevelt. Glendon writes:

> The working group was instructed to propose a logical arrangement of the articles supplied by the Secretariat, to redraft them on the basis of suggestions from the drafting committee, and to make recommendations concerning what articles should be in the Declaration and what should be placed in the Covenant.[11]

THE CASSIN DRAFT

The subcommittee decided that the work should be tackled by one person, and then reviewed by the rest. Because he was both a legal scholar and an excellent writer, Cassin was charged with

(continues on page 58)

EXCERPTS FROM THE UNIVERSAL DECLARATION OF HUMAN RIGHTS

PREAMBLE

Whereas recognition of the inherent dignity and of the equal and inalienable rights of all members of the human family is the foundation of freedom, justice and peace in the world,

Whereas disregard and contempt for human rights have resulted in barbarous acts which have outraged the conscience of mankind, and the advent of a world in which human beings shall enjoy freedom of speech and belief and freedom from fear and want has been proclaimed as the highest aspiration of the common people,

Whereas it is essential, if man is not to be compelled to have recourse, as a last resort, to rebellion against tyranny and oppression, that human rights should be protected by the rule of law,

Whereas it is essential to promote the development of friendly relations between nations,

Whereas the peoples of the United Nations have in the Charter reaffirmed their faith in fundamental human rights, in the dignity and worth of the human person and in the equal rights of men and women and have determined to promote social progress and better standards of life in larger freedom,

Whereas Member States have pledged themselves to achieve, in cooperation with the United Nations, the promotion of universal respect for and observance of human rights and fundamental freedoms,

Whereas a common understanding of these rights and freedoms is of the greatest importance for the full realization of this pledge,

Now, therefore, The General Assembly proclaims This Universal Declaration of Human Rights as a common standard of achievement for all peoples and all nations, to the end that every individual and every organ of society, keeping this Declaration constantly in mind, shall strive by teaching and education to promote respect for these rights and freedoms and by progressive measures, national and international, to secure their universal and effective recognition and observance, both among the peoples of Member States themselves and among the peoples of territories under their jurisdiction.

ARTICLE 1
All human beings are born free and equal in dignity and rights. They are endowed with reason and conscience and should act towards one another in a spirit of brotherhood.

ARTICLE 2
Everyone is entitled to all the rights and freedoms set forth in this Declaration, without distinction of any kind, such as race, colour, sex, language, religion, political or other opinion, national or social origin, property, birth or other status. . . .

ARTICLE 3
Everyone has the right to life, liberty and security of person.

ARTICLE 4
No one shall be held in slavery or servitude; slavery and the slave trade shall be prohibited in all their forms.

ARTICLE 5
No one shall be subjected to torture or to cruel, inhuman or degrading treatment or punishment. . . .

ARTICLE 9
No one shall be subjected to arbitrary arrest, detention or exile. . . .

ARTICLE 14
(1) Everyone has the right to seek and to enjoy in other countries asylum from persecution.

(continues)

(continued)

(2) This right may not be invoked in the case of prosecutions genuinely arising from non-political crimes or from acts contrary to the purposes and principles of the United Nations.

ARTICLE 15

(1) Everyone has the right to a nationality.

(2) No one shall be arbitrarily deprived of his nationality nor denied the right to change his nationality.

ARTICLE 16

(1) Men and women of full age, without any limitation due to race, nationality or religion, have the right to marry and to found a family. They are entitled to equal rights as to marriage, during marriage and at its dissolution.

(2) Marriage shall be entered into only with the free and full consent of the intending spouses.

(3) The family is the natural and fundamental group unit of society and is entitled to protection by society and the State. . . .

ARTICLE 18

Everyone has the right to freedom of thought, conscience and religion; this right includes freedom to change his religion or belief, and freedom, either alone or in community with others and in public or private, to manifest his religion or belief in teaching, practice, worship and observance. . . .

ARTICLE 25

(1) Everyone has the right to a standard of living adequate for the health and well-being of himself and of his

(continued from page 55)

this task. Cassin was, at the time, head of the *Conseil d'Etat*, the highest court in France, and had helped rebuild France's judicial system after the war's end.

The second draft, known as the Cassin draft, was completed in two days, in June 1947. Cassin reorganized the Humphrey draft and revised it in several ways. In addition to adding a family, including food, clothing, housing and medical care and necessary social services, and the right to security in the event of unemployment, sickness, disability, widowhood, old age or other lack of livelihood in circumstances beyond his control.

(2) Motherhood and childhood are entitled to special care and assistance. All children, whether born in or out of wedlock, shall enjoy the same social protection.

ARTICLE 26

(1) Everyone has the right to education. Education shall be free, at least in the elementary and fundamental stages. Elementary education shall be compulsory. Technical and professional education shall be made generally available and higher education shall be equally accessible to all on the basis of merit.

(2) Education shall be directed to the full development of the human personality and to the strengthening of respect for human rights and fundamental freedoms. It shall promote understanding, tolerance and friendship among all nations, racial or religious groups, and shall further the activities of the United Nations for the maintenance of peace.

(3) Parents have a prior right to choose the kind of education that shall be given to their children. . . .*

---

* G.A. res. 217A (III), U.N. Doc A/810 at 71 (1948), Adopted on December 10, 1948, by the General Assembly of the United Nations (without dissent).

preamble, he included "six introductory articles, thirty-six substantive articles grouped analytically under eight headings, and two concluding provisions on implementation."[12] According to Glendon, Cassin's biggest contribution was providing the Humphrey draft with a more accessible organization and making it logically consistent and sound. While the Humphrey draft had tackled the issues by topic, the Cassin draft shaped them in a way that provided a reason for the document (the preamble), as well as arranged the rights according to principles, rather than in a random way.

The revision was a success. Glendon notes, "Though the document would undergo many further changes over the next year and a half, most of the ideas in Humphrey's draft ultimately found their way into the Universal Declaration, and the 'logical arrangement' contributed by Cassin held firm."[13]

An unfortunate problem would arise later, however, about the authorship of the Declaration of Human Rights. For years, Cassin was credited as its chief author (he was even referred to as its father), and Humphrey's pivotal role in writing the first draft was ignored or unknown. It also does not seem that Cassin tried to set the record straight about the drafting of the document. Although Humphrey never complained, his role eventually became known decades later, after researchers uncovered a draft of the original declaration in his own handwriting among his papers. Ever humble, he insisted when the discovery was made that "to say I did the draft alone would be nonsense. . . . The final Declaration was the work of hundreds."[14]

One of the most important parts of Cassin's revision, as stated before, is the inclusion of the preamble, which described the reasons why the declaration had become necessary. Organized into six parts, it states: "Ignorance and contempt of human rights have been among the principal causes of the suffering of humanity and particularly of the massacres which have polluted the earth in two world wars." It also asserted, in the second part, "There can be no peace unless human rights and freedoms are respected."[15]

Although these words were later revised, their essential message was preserved in the final draft. This was important in order to establish the need for the document as well as to prevent criticism by nations that might question the UN's role in undertaking the task of producing such a document.

Lingering Debates

REVISING THE CASSIN DRAFT

Despite the improved structure of the document, the Cassin draft still needed further revision before it would meet with final approval. Cassin presented it to the drafting subcommittee on June 17, 1947. Over the next week, the group discussed several priorities, including their ability to complete both the declaration *and* a covenant before the deadline of the fall of 1948. Eleanor Roosevelt, in view of time constraints, said that "the Committee might have to choose between a completed draft of a Declaration and a completed draft of a Convention."[1] As the group began its review of Cassin's draft, it became clear that there would be no time to work on a convention draft as well. By the time the drafting subcommittee concluded its meeting, it had made some changes to Cassin's draft, but several issues still loomed. These would be brought before the larger commission when the draft was presented to them.

That second meeting of the full Human Rights Commission was held in Geneva, Switzerland, in December 1947. Although she anticipated many long, intricate debates, Roosevelt wrote that she also hoped for "something tangible [to be] accomplished that may be of value in the future."[2] Roosevelt's famous work ethic came into play during the Geneva session: She was determined that the meeting would be productive, and to ensure that outcome, she established a work schedule that included long days as well as night sessions. The 18 members of the commission joked with her that their own human rights were being violated by her rigor, but she remained adamant that their work would be concluded—and concluded effectively—before the end of the session on December 17. They abided by her schedule, although on one or more occasions they rebelled against her strict scheduling. Once the group showed up for a late-night work session half an hour late and drunk. Because they had enjoyed too many drinks during dinner, she was forced to cancel the meeting and the items on the agenda until the following day. For the most part, however, the group worked diligently through its review of the Cassin draft, and the debates were lively and often heated.

IMPLEMENTATION OF THE DECLARATION

The commission again took up the issue of how the declaration would be implemented or enforced. Hansa Mehta and William Hodgson, the Indian and Australian representatives respectively, asserted that the declaration would be meaningless without a method of enforcement and were likely upset by the drafting subcommittee's unofficial decision to delay work on the draft of a covenant, which would be a binding legal document. Again, Mehta and Hodgson encouraged the committee to consider several alternatives, such as the recom-

René Cassin and Eleanor Roosevelt talk during a meeting of the UN Commission on Human Rights held in Geneva, Switzerland, in December 1947.

mendation by the commission of establishing an international tribunal, or the drafting of a convention or covenant in addition to a declaration.

It was, as Charles Malik later noted, a debate between the larger nations and the smaller ones. Many smaller nations that were members of the UN had recently come into existence or been liberated as former colonies. Having endured years of oppression and colonialism, they feared that a declaration alone would be empty. They hoped that a stronger document or method of implementation of the human rights listed would offer a legal precedent for their own nations as their new governments took shape. The larger nations, however, feared interference from the international community into their domestic affairs.

Fernand Dehousse, of Belgium, proposed that the commission work simultaneously in subcommittees on the development of all three items: a final declaration draft, a covenant, and implementation methods. The commission's members accepted this as a compromise and divided the work among three subcommittees, which would take a few days and report to the larger group by December 12. When the larger group reconvened, however, the reports of the covenant and implementation subcommittees were met with fierce debate. It became obvious that the main problem was not in drafting a declaration, but in determining how to enforce it. By the end of the session, the most substantive outcome was a solid discussion of the declaration, which had been worked upon by Roosevelt, Cassin, and others.

GENDER ISSUES

Issues of gender equality arose in the committee's debates at several points. For example, in discussing the Cassin draft, Mehta suggested that the use of the term *man* rather than a nonexclusive term such as *person* or *human being* should be reconsidered. She worried that some countries would use the term *man* as a justification for excluding women from benefiting from the rights listed. Roosevelt, the other woman on the commission, disagreed, saying that everyone essentially understood that *man* was a term that referred to all people. Unlike Roosevelt, notes Mary Ann Glendon, Mehta was "battling back home [in India] against purdah [the practice of keeping women from being seen by men], child marriage, polygamy, unequal inheritance laws, and bans on marriages among different castes, striving to set these ancient customs on a course of extinction."[3] The term was not changed to a more general one, which would make Mehta unhappy (though it would be changed later, during other revisions, before being finalized).

In relation to women's rights, the issue of whether it was a human right to be married or not came up. The Secretariat's draft had included the right to marriage, and Cassin had added a special clause listing the need for the state to offer protection to women and children—the reason being that children and women were sometimes vulnerable members of society. They also added a specific clause that, in cases of divorce, women and men had equal rights.

THE INDIVIDUAL VERSUS THE STATE

One of the most essential issues—and one that had been brewing for some time in the various phases of the declaration's drafting—was the question of individual rights versus those of the "common good," or larger population. The reason the issue was so pivotal was that it reflected the difference in ideology between the Western democratic nations, like the United States and Great Britain, and the Soviet Union and those Soviet-influenced Eastern nations with Communist governments.

For Western states, the rights of individuals took priority over those of the larger society. The civil and political rights of freedom of speech, religion, and the press, among others, were vital to maintaining order within society and in preventing the government from abusing or oppressing its citizens. The Soviets claimed that individual rights were also important to them, but from a socialist perspective—an individual could not enjoy those civil and political rights if the nation's economy and military were not strong and effective. In other words, individual rights were not feasible if the state were not strong enough to provide and enforce them. Therefore, rights such as the right to work, the right to fair housing, the right to health care, and the like were central to the Soviet-bloc nations. Although it was thought that the issue had been initially resolved in other sessions by deciding to include *both* civil and political rights as well as social and economic rights to the declaration, the debate continued to rage.

By this point in the process, the Soviet Union had changed its representative on the Human Rights Commission several times. In Geneva, its representative was Alexander Bogomolov, who worked diligently, but whose reports back to the Soviet foreign office stressed the need for the Soviets to produce their own draft of a declaration for presentation at a later date. Roosevelt's skills as chair of the commission were heavily taxed during these debates, although she later wrote that she was certain compromise would eventually be reached:

> One of the questions I'm most frequently asked is whether I think we can produce a draft on which the Eastern European group and the United States can agree. I think this is quite possible. They like a greater emphasis on the authority of the state, and when it comes to social and economic rights they are most anxious to spell them out in detail. The rights and freedoms of the individual, and religious and spiritual questions, don't seem to them as important in a draft of this kind. But certainly a balance can be reached.[4]

Later, Roosevelt's frustrations would show; in fact, as the declaration continued to progress through the chain of approvals it needed, she would accuse the Soviets of attempting to kill the declaration outright. In a 1948 speech in Paris, she noted that the Soviets prided themselves on their ability to guarantee every citizen the right to work and often accused other nations, especially the United States, of having high unemployment rates. Roosevelt pointed out that Soviet citizens often did not have any say in where or how they work. "A society in which everyone works is not necessarily a free society," she said, "and may indeed be a slave society. . . . We in the United States have come to realize [the right to work] means freedom to choose one's job, to work or not to work as one desires."[5] Her comments highlight the tension between the priority of the individual's rights over that of the state and vice versa. Although tensions would continue to crop up in both the Geneva debates and others, she remained hopeful that all parties could agree on a final draft.

Overcoming
Hurdles

APPROACHING A FINAL DRAFT

When the meetings in Geneva adjourned, Roosevelt was happy with the progress the commission had made on Cassin's draft. The drafting committee agreed to meet again in New York in early May 1948 to prepare a final draft to be discussed at the full commission's third meeting, which would be held later that same month. The draft in hand was now being referred to as the Geneva draft, after the changes that had been included to Cassin's version during the second full commission meeting.

In New York that May, the drafting committee settled down to complete its work. The members of the committee wanted to finalize the draft by focusing on the specific wording, clarifying the language to make it accessible to and acceptable by the largest number of nations possible; in other words, they wanted to make the language as universal as possible.

By this time, feedback from other nations was filtering in to the group, which proved both illuminating and frustrating. Many of the suggestions were ones that the full commission had already debated in depth and was not eager to resume. Other nations had very specific items they wanted to be included, which reflected their own situations: Egypt, for example, wanted it to be clarified that "economic and social rights could be exercised only insofar as the economic conditions of each state permitted,"[1] because its leaders feared it could not financially provide for each of its citizens. Other nations worried about the compatibility of the rights listed with their own laws and traditions: Some Islamic states worried about the right to change one's religion, because according to their own laws, abandoning Islam for another religion or for atheism (known as apostasy) was considered a crime; Sweden was also concerned about the religion clause because it had a law at the time forbidding any member of the Swedish State Church from leaving it.

Roosevelt's practical side helped to establish some guidelines for the drafting committee. She encouraged them to focus only on specific articles, rather than on general principles and broad ideas, so that they could present as complete a final draft as possible to the full commission. Their work, however, would be complicated by the outbreak of war in the Middle East between the Arab nations and the newly formed state of Israel in May 1948. This development especially impacted member Charles Malik, whose home nation of Lebanon was on the northern border of the Israeli-Palestinian disputed territory. The outbreak of war created tension between Malik and Cassin. As a Jew who had lost many family members in the Holocaust, Cassin supported the creation of a Jewish state. Although he sympathized with the plight of the Jewish people, Malik, like many Arabs, rejected the idea of establishing a new state in the midst of a territory already populated by Arabs.

Another complication was the presence of the new Soviet delegate, Alexei Pavlov, who had replaced the easygoing and genial Bogomolov. At the outset of the meeting on May 3, Pavlov suggested that the Geneva draft be put aside and that the committee begin work on a totally new draft. This appalled most members, especially Roosevelt. Although this idea was rejected, it set the tone for the difficulties that the group would encounter in working with Pavlov. Roosevelt especially had a tense experience with him, as many of his comments focused on direct comparisons between the treatment by the Soviet Union and the United States of its own people; he referred to the continued discrimination of African Americans by the U.S. government and to the housing conditions of some Americans in urban slums. As Mary Ann Glendon notes, "Pavlov, even more than the Soviet delegates who preceded him, put a strain on Mrs. Roosevelt's legendary people skills."[2]

Time and time again, rather than allow the group to focus on the specific wording of articles as Roosevelt had encouraged them to do, Pavlov returned to broader issues and principles, which caused so many delays that the drafting committee had not completed its review of the entire document by the May 21 deadline. When the full commission's third meeting began on May 24, with an agenda to review the full draft and prepare it to be sent for approval to the United Nations Economic and Social Council (ECOSOC), Pavlov again held up the proceedings. The representatives from Ukraine and Belarus were not present because of visa issues for entering the United States, and an angered Pavlov insisted that the meeting not proceed without them. Thus, two full days were wasted waiting for the representatives. When the commission's meeting finally got underway, it was on a sour note.

"THE MOST DIFFICULT STAGE"

Getting through the draft proved tedious and difficult. John Humphrey later wrote that this was inevitable: "We are, of course, in the most difficult stage. In the past, it was largely individuals who were expressing their opinions and making their decisions . . . The tendency in the past, moreover, was to slide over difficulties, to put them off; these must now be faced."[3]

Pavlov had certainly received instructions from his government to delay proceedings and now "proposed amendments to almost every article,"[4] Glendon notes. For example, when it came to many of the individual rights listed, he wanted to add statements like "in accordance with the law of the State," a suggestion that concerned other members who pointed out that many nations—as Germany had done before and during World War II—could easily pass laws that infringed upon or obstructed those rights listed. Pavlov also insisted that the duties of individuals to the state should be included; for example, he felt that individuals owed certain allegiances and had responsibilities to their homelands to make those nations strong, which should be listed, but the committee felt this was too unwieldy a topic to tackle at this late stage. Thus, Pavlov's ideas went unsupported by the others, and in the end, the support of the Soviets for the declaration was lost.

Despite the jousting with Pavlov, the meeting was successful. In the end, the Egyptian and British representatives suggested a statement that the social and economic rights would be implemented "in accordance with the organization and resources of each State," which put to rest the concerns of still-emerging nations that feared they would be in violation of the declaration because their financial resources prevented the provision of education, social security, adequate housing, and so forth to all citizens. Malik prepared a draft of a revised preamble, in which he emphasized the need for such a declaration of human rights as well as clarified the purpose of the

(continues on page 74)

FOREWORD OF *BROKEN PROMISES*, A 2008 REPORT BY AMNESTY INTERNATIONAL

The international human rights organization Amnesty International published a report on the sixtieth anniversary of the Universal Declaration of Human Rights, criticizing the lack of effort by world leaders and national governments on human rights issues. An excerpt from the report's foreword follows:

> World leaders owe an apology for failing to deliver on the promise of justice and equality in the Universal Declaration of Human Rights (UDHR), adopted 60 years ago. In the past six decades, many governments have shown more interest in the abuse of power or in the pursuit of political self-interest, than in respecting the rights of those they lead.
>
> This is not to deny the progress that has been made in developing human rights standards, systems and institutions internationally, regionally and nationally. . . . More countries today provide constitutional and legal protection for human rights than ever before. Only a handful of states would openly deny the right of the international community to scrutinize their human rights records. 2007 saw the first full year of operation of the UN Human Rights Council, through which all UN member states have agreed to a public debate on their human rights performance. But for all the good, the fact remains that injustice, inequality and impunity are still the hallmarks of our world today.
>
> In 1948, . . . world leaders came together to adopt the UDHR [Universal Declaration of Human Rights]. Member states of the fledgling UN showed great fore-

sight and courage by putting their faith in global values. They were acutely aware of the horrors of World War II, and conscious of the grim realities of an emerging Cold War. Their vision was not circumscribed by what was happening only in Europe. 1948 was also the year in which Burma gained independence, Mahatma Gandhi was assassinated, and apartheid laws were first introduced in South Africa. Large parts of the world were still under the yoke of colonization.

The drafters of the UDHR acted out of the conviction that only a multilateral system of global values, based on equality, justice and the rule of law, could stand up to the challenges ahead. In a genuine exercise of leadership, they resisted the pressure from competing political camps. . . . They recognized that the universality of human rights—every person is born free and equal—and their indivisibility . . . is the basis for our collective security as well as our common humanity. In the years that followed, visionary leadership gave way to narrow political interests. Human rights became a divisive game as the two "superpowers" engaged in an ideological and geopolitical struggle to establish their supremacy. One side denied civil and political rights, while the other demoted economic and social rights. Human rights were used as a tool to further strategic ends, rather than to promote people's dignity and welfare. Newly independent countries, caught in the superpower competition, struggled in the pursuit of democracy and the rule of law or abandoned them altogether for various forms of authoritarianism.

Hopes for human rights rose with the end of the Cold War but were dashed by the explosion of ethnic conflicts and implosion of states that unleashed a spate of humanitarian emergencies, marked by massive and vicious human rights abuses. . . .

As we entered the 21st century, the terrorist attacks of 11 September 2001 transformed the human rights debate

(continues)

(continued)

> yet again into a divisive and destructive one between "western" and "non-western," restricting liberties, fuelling suspicion, fear, discrimination and prejudice among governments and peoples alike.
>
> The forces of economic globalization brought new promises, but also challenges. Though world leaders claimed to commit themselves to eradicating poverty, for the most part they ignored the human rights abuses that drive and deepen poverty. The UDHR remained a paper promise. . . .
>
> The political landscape today is very different from that of 60 years ago. There are many more states today than in 1948. Some former colonies are now emerging as global players alongside their former colonial masters. Can we expect the old and new powers to come together, as their predecessors did in 1948, and recommit themselves to human rights?*

---

* *Broken Promises.* Amnesty International, 2008. http://the report.amnesty.org/document/47.

(continued from page 71)
document as a declaration of goals toward which all nations should work. With some revisions, the commission accepted the preamble. On June 18, the full commission voted on the declaration itself. It was approved, 12–0, with the Soviet Union, the Ukraine, and Belarus abstaining.

The declaration was ready for the next phases: to be approved by ECOSOC, then by the Third Committee on Social, Humanitarian and Cultural Affairs, and finally by the UN General Assembly. Luckily for the commission, the new president of ECOSOC was none other than Charles Malik. Later, he would also chair the Third Committee as well.

PROGRESS

"The year 1948," Malik later wrote, "witnessed the oddest coincidence of my life at the United Nations." Glendon notes, "The delegate from tiny Lebanon was wearing three big hats as the Declaration moved through its crucial final stages in the fall of 1948."[5] Malik had impressed his colleagues at the United Nations as a practical-minded intellectual who was effective and efficient in pursuing the work of the international organization.

His position as head of ECOSOC during the time that the draft on the declaration of human rights was to be presented to that body was fortuitous. Many of ECOSOC's members were diplomats who were sometimes dismissive of the need for a human rights statement. Other issues took priority in their minds, such as economic points. Indeed, the Soviet Union's representative to ECOSOC was none other than Pavlov, who was sure to use this sentiment among other members to delay the draft and stall its progress to the next round.

The human rights declaration was only one of many issues on ECOSOC's agenda when it met in mid-July 1948. Perhaps sensing the lack of concern ECOSOC representatives had for human rights, chairman Malik allowed the other issues on the agenda to take up much of the council's time. In fact, when they finally turned to a review of the declaration, ECOSOC decided that it had too little time for detailed discussion and voted unanimously simply to pass it through to the Third Committee. One big hurdle, thanks to Malik's foresight and cunning, had been overcome.

On September 28, 1948, the next hurdle was approached. When the Third Committee convened in Paris to review the human rights declaration, Roosevelt formally presented the declaration. In her opening statement, she noted that the draft was not absolutely perfect. She and the others who had worked on it worried that approval would be delayed if the Third Committee members tried to tinker with the language of every individual article, which would probably occur again in the General

Assembly. If approval were delayed in the Third Committee, the declaration would have to wait another year to be presented to the General Assembly. She encouraged the Third Committee to remember that the declaration would undergo more revisions and that its focus should be larger issues and not a "search for absolute perfection."[6]

Despite Roosevelt's pleas, she was upset to see that the Third Committee's members began debating, as she put it, "every single word of that draft declaration over and over again."[7] For example, it took several days just to discuss general ideas, and then six days just to complete a discussion of Article I. Unlike Roosevelt, Malik, who presided over the meeting, which lasted many, many days, was not disturbed or alarmed by this. He understood that many of the smaller nations, especially those that had emerged or been established after World War II, had a lot at stake and needed to voice their concerns. He also knew that if members did not voice their concerns, they would be less likely in the end to support approval of the declaration.

Several other threats to approval presented themselves. Almost immediately, some nations raised the issue of implementation. How would the rights listed be implemented by individual nations? How would they be enforced if the declaration were to be nonbinding? Some states suggested delaying a vote on the declaration until a draft of a covenant was also ready so the two would be considered together; this, however, would surely have destroyed any chance of submitting the declaration that year to the General Assembly. Fortunately for Roosevelt and her fellow committee members, the motion was not passed.

Other issues that arose included the concerns of some nations about whether the declaration would allow the international community to interfere with a nation's sovereignty. One big issue related to the origin of human rights: Were human beings entitled to human rights because they were God given, or were those rights inherent in human nature?

A photo of the complete text of the Universal Declaration of Human Rights. Getting not only the drafting committee, but also the entire UN General Assembly to approve the final language of the declaration would prove to be a monumental task.

Still other nations questioned the idea that the list of rights, many of them gleaned from documents such as the Declaration of Independence and the Declaration of the Rights of Man, reflected Western values and were therefore not applicable to all the countries present who would need to approve it. This idea was countered effectively by P.C. Chang, who emphasized that broadly international sources had been consulted and how careful the committee had been to ensure the universality of the rights it included. Not surprisingly, Pavlov and the other Soviet-friendly nations did whatever they could to perpetuate debate and disagreement.

John Humphrey's letter to his sister (composed during one of the discussion sessions) shows the frustration he felt:

> I am writing this letter during a session of the Third Committee of the General Assembly. I suppose I should be listening to the South American gentleman who is expounding on Article 3 of the Declaration of Human Rights, but I have heard so many of these speeches that it is only in revolt that I can hope to find sanity. We have been on this thing for 3 weeks now and have adopted 2 out of the 28 articles. When we will finish Lord only knows.[8]

THE THIRD COMMITTEE GIVES ITS APPROVAL

After a month of debate, only three articles had been completely discussed and approved. Malik then imposed a time limit on speeches and scheduled night sessions as well, to make sure the declaration would be ready for the UN General Assembly meeting in December. The strategy helped, and the work picked up in pace; with morning, afternoon, and night meetings, the Third Committee completed discussion of roughly one article per day.

The title of the document, which had been referred to at this point as the International Declaration of Human Rights, was changed to the Universal Declaration of Human Rights.

The change had been proposed by Cassin, who wanted it to be clear that the declaration "was not an 'international' or 'inter-governmental' document," explains Glendon, but that "it was addressed to all humanity and founded on a unified conception of the human being."[9] It was imperative that all people everywhere recognize the rights, not just governments.

After two solid months of work and over 80 meetings, the Third Committee approved the Universal Declaration of Human Rights on December 7, 1948, at three o'clock in the morning. Seven nations had abstained, including, unsurprisingly, all the Soviet-friendly nations.

It was now ready to for the final hurdle—approval by the United Nations General Assembly.

Approval and Success

THE GENERAL ASSEMBLY VOTES

The General Assembly meeting convened in early December 1948. The draft of the Universal Declaration of Human Rights would require two-thirds of the vote to gain approval. The mood was tense, as Roosevelt, Malik, Chang, Cassin, Santa Cruz, and the others hoped that their two years of hard work would not prove fruitless.

Charles Malik, rather than Eleanor Roosevelt, formally presented the declaration to the General Assembly on December 9 for consideration. It is likely the committee felt he should do so because of the pivotal role he had played in shepherding the document through ECOSOC as well as the exhausting Third Committee. His reputation at the UN by this point was also quite prestigious, and many in the world body regarded him with respect and admiration.

In his memorable speech, Malik stressed that the declaration was the product of many hands from many nations and walks of life. He also pointed out the history that would be made should it be passed. He also stated his aspirations for the declaration, insisting that it would "serve as a potent critic of existing practice. It will help to transform reality." He added, "Every member of the United Nations has solemnly pledged itself to achieve respect for and observance of human rights. But, precisely what these rights are we were never told before, either in the Charter or in any other international instrument. This is the first time the principles of human rights and fundamental freedoms are spelled out authoritatively and in precise detail." If the document were approved, Malik noted, any person objecting to his or her government's actions would have "the moral support of the entire world."[1]

Chang, Cassin, and Roosevelt also made speeches in support of the declaration before the General Assembly. In hers, Roosevelt said, "This Declaration may well become the international Magna Carta of all men everywhere" and would inspire people around the world "to a higher standard of life and to a greater enjoyment of freedom."[2]

Many other delegates addressed the General Assembly on the issue of the declaration, including Roosevelt's old nemesis, Andrey Vyshinsky who, along with other delegates from the Soviet bloc, tried to delay the declaration until the next meeting of the General Assembly by attacking the United States and rehashing the idea that the declaration was not yet complete as it did not suitably address state sovereignty and other issues.

Voting began around midnight on December 10. Forty-eight nations voted in favor of it, none opposed, and eight abstained, including the Soviet Union. The Universal Declaration of Human Rights had been passed and approved by the United Nations.

Charles Malik addresses the Japanese Peace Conference in October 1951. Malik's impassioned presentation of the Universal Declaration of Human Rights to the UN General Assembly helped secure its passage.

Lois Scharf notes, when the tally was complete, "the delegates rose in unison to give Eleanor Roosevelt an ovation."[3] Others spoke admiringly of her dedication and care in moving the declaration through its many phases and manifestations.

Charles Malik was also exuberant. He later said: "Whoever values man and his individual freedom above everything else cannot fail to find in the present Declaration a potent ideological weapon. If wielded in complete goodwill, sincerity, and truth, this weapon can prove most significant in the history of the spirit."[4]

Others were not so positive, including the Soviets. Andrey Vyshinsky, no fan of Eleanor Roosevelt and her circle, blasted the approval as an attempt by Western powers to intervene in the domestic affairs of other nations, such as those with Communist governments.[5]

There was still much reason to celebrate. Scharf writes: "The Universal Declaration of Human Rights was a great personal achievement, but Eleanor was both modest and realistic about the work she had guided and pushed to completion. Written affirmations of human dignity and rights were words, not realities." Roosevelt wrote to her aunt that while the document was a standard "to which all men may aspire & which we should try to achieve," nonetheless "it had no legal value but should carry moral weight."[6]

There was still much work to be done to make sure the efforts of Roosevelt and her team would not be in vain.

THE FATE OF THE TEAM

After the declaration's passage, the leaders of the commission remained active in the field of human rights. In addition to working on behalf of the Democratic Party, Eleanor Roosevelt continued to fight for human rights. After resigning her position as delegate to the United Nations in 1952, she aided the growing U.S. civil rights movement, particularly by publicly supporting the Montgomery bus boycott in 1955, the leaders of which advocated desegregating the public transportation system. In 1961, President John F. Kennedy reappointed her to the United Nations; that same year she also chaired the Presidential Commission on the Status of Women. When Eleanor Roosevelt died on November 7, 1962, at the age of 78, the world mourned her passing. She was remembered as a true leader, a woman who had come into her own both during and after her husband's administration, and whose life had been spent working toward the goal of improving life for people all over the world.

René Cassin, who had been instrumental in working on the declaration, continued to have a long and distinguished career in human rights advocacy. In 1968, he won the Nobel Peace Prize, the year of the twentieth anniversary of the approval of the Universal Declaration of Human Rights. In its announcement of the prize, the Nobel Prize Committee cited the work of Cassin on the drafting committee of the Human Rights Commission:

> In [the committee's] extremely laborious work, in which each and every concept and the validity of each and every word were thoroughly aired in all languages, Professor Cassin held a key position. He formulated, defined, and clarified. He was crystal clear in his formulations and steadfast in his goal, but always cooperative and tolerant of the opinions of others.[7]

Despite the accolades, Cassin was still unhappy with how the declaration had been implemented 20 years later. In an article written in 1968, he said bluntly: "Now that we possess an instrument capable of lifting or easing the burden of oppression and injustice in the world, we must learn to use it."[8] Cassin died on February 20, 1976.

Although Charles Malik was admired for his work in human rights, he continued to be personally troubled by problems in the Middle East stemming from the ongoing Israeli-Palestinian conflict. After leaving politics, he resumed a teaching career, and he maintained his residence in Beirut during the Lebanese

Civil War, which lasted from 1975 to 1990. Malik had been popular during his career, but some of his positions—such as his opinion that Jerusalem should be an international city rather than governed exclusively by either Arabs or Israelis—made him unpopular in many circles. He died on December 28, 1987.

P.C. Chang's time on the Human Rights Commission had been difficult because his home country, China, was in the midst of a civil war between nationalist and Communist forces. On October 1, 1949, Mao Zedong, the Communist Party leader, declared the country the People's Republic of China. In the years that followed, China became increasingly militaristic and isolated from other nations, a change sure to upset the scholar whose strength on the commission was in finding the commonality between cultures. A tireless promoter of Chinese culture and ideas, Chang grew disappointed with the turn of events in his native country. He died in 1957.

THE ROLE OF NONGOVERNMENTAL ORGANIZATIONS

Eleanor Roosevelt always said that the passing of the Universal Declaration of Human Rights had been one of her greatest personal successes. Before she died in 1962, she witnessed the development of a substantial human rights movement. The emergence of this movement is often credited to the existence of the Universal Declaration of Human Rights. Robert G. Patman notes, "The status of the Universal Declaration is unique. Unlike other significant documents such as the Magna Carta, the French Declaration of the Rights of Man and the American Declaration of Independence, it is concerned with the rights and freedoms of people everywhere."[9] It is the first statement of its kind asserting the fundamental rights of human beings no matter where they live and without regard to which race, ethnic group, religion, or geographic entity they belong. According to Jacqueline Langwith, "The Universal Declaration of Human Rights provides the basic foundation of human rights law, declaring that all humans have certain inalienable rights."[10] In other words, it is important as a document because it established a legal precedent for future laws and covenants related to the topic of human rights.

During the Cold War between the Eastern and Western powers, human rights as an international political issue did not blossom as it might have. For more than 40 years, it always took a backseat to the main concern of the day: the proliferation of nuclear weapons and the competition between the superpowers, the United States and the Soviet Union. Yet during that time, progress was made in many other ways, such as in the establishment of several human rights organizations. Patman, writing about the rise of many nongovernmental organizations during the Cold War, notes: "Amnesty International, which was founded in 1961 and received the Nobel Peace Prize in 1977, became perhaps the best-known such organization."[11]

Amnesty International describes itself as "a worldwide movement of people who campaign for internationally recognized human rights for all."[12] It claims over 2 million members in over 150 countries who work to advocate human rights in various ways, such as by making abuses of these rights public, by campaigning to end violations, and by conducting research to document abuses of human rights. Among their priorities are violence against women, the death penalty, the imprisonment of political dissenters, torture, and the rights of refugees.

Amnesty's work is not easy, of course, especially in light of the ongoing abuses of imprisoned people around the world. According to a survey conducted in 1994 by the Redress Trust, 123 out of the 185 nations that are members of the United Nations do torture or mistreat their prisoners.[13] Indeed, Amnesty International often publishes reports in which it criticizes governments around the world for violating the rights of their own citizens.

Human Rights Watch, founded in 1978, is the largest human rights advocacy organization based in the United States. An independent organization, it describes its mission in the following way: "By focusing international attention where human rights are violated, we give voice to the oppressed and hold oppressors accountable for their crimes. Our rigorous, objective investigations and strategic, targeted advocacy build intense pressure for action and raise the cost of human rights abuse."[14] It was an active participant in drafting the Rome Statute, which led to the creation of the International Criminal Court. Presented in 1998 and ratified four years later, the statute establishes an international, permanent court for trying people accused of acts of genocide and other crimes against humanity.

Another prominent organization is Doctors Without Borders, or *Médecins Sans Frontières* (MSF), which was established in France in 1971 by doctors and journalists. Comprising approximately 30,000 doctors, nurses, administrators, and other medical professionals, MSF's mission is to provide medical aid to people who otherwise are unable to receive it due to conditions of war, epidemics, natural disasters, or governmental oppression. Its mission has other dimensions, as well; MSF declares its organization "reserves the right to speak out to bring attention to neglected crises, to challenge inadequacies or abuse of the aid system, and to advocate for improved medical treatments and protocols."[15] The organization does not involve itself in politics by taking sides on issues, but rather focuses solely on providing relief to populations in most desperate need. It does, however, bring public awareness to human rights violations that are the cause of medical disasters and injustices, such as unaddressed poverty and armed conflict. For example, MSF called for military intervention during the 1994 genocide in Rwanda, in which almost a million Tutsis were massacred in just 100 days.

Nongovernmental organizations such as these and countless others serve the global human rights agenda not only by working to address human rights violations but also by documenting such abuses. Their work helps to hold those who are responsible—be they individuals or governments—accountable.

9

The Impact of the Declaration

IMPLEMENTATION OF THE UNIVERSAL DECLARATION

One of the issues that had plagued the Human Rights Commission during the drafting process had been whether or not the declaration would have any "teeth"—any measures of implementation. Even after the document had been approved by the UN General Assembly on December 10, 1948, Roosevelt still mused, "I wondered whether a mere statement of rights, without legal obligation, would inspire governments to see that these rights were observed."[1]

Measures to assure implementation would follow, but not for another three decades. Two covenants, the International Covenant on Civil and Political Rights and the International

Covenant on Economic, Social and Cultural Rights, were worked on by none other than René Cassin and formally presented to the United Nations in 1966. (They went into effect a decade later, in 1976, because the covenants first had to be ratified by individual member states.) Together with the declaration itself, these covenants form what is referred to as the International Bill of Rights. The nations that have ratified them are expected to abide by them, although whether or not this happens is often a cause of controversy regarding the UN's present role in world affairs.

Four additional documents that built upon the declaration have also been passed: the United Nations Convention on the Rights of the Child; the Convention Against Torture and Other Cruel, Inhuman or Degrading Treatment or Punishment; the International Convention on the Elimination of All Forms of Racial Discrimination; and the Convention on the Elimination of All Forms of Discrimination Against Women. Together, these six "elaborate particular rights, set standards, and specify the rights of certain groups of people,"[2] according to Jacqueline Langwith.

TEHRAN

In 1968—the year that Cassin won the Nobel Peace Prize for his work in drafting the declaration 20 years earlier—the United Nations held its first International Conference on Human Rights in Tehran, Iran. The landmark meeting was, by some accounts, successful, but most found it to be a tense occasion that dealt a critical blow to the progress being made on human rights.

According to Roland Burke, the tension at the conference was caused by the "altered balance of forces in the UN following decolonization and the decisive role played by the non-Western states."[3] In the 20 years since the declaration had been approved, many Asian, African, and other countries had been liberated from Western colonization and had joined the UN's General Assembly, which made the majority of nations in the assembly non-Western. (Since the formation of the UN in 1945, Western nations had been in the majority). For the first time, Burke says, "the greatest global powers in the world were having the diplomatic agenda dictated to them by a collection of militarily weak and economically impoverished states."[4]

Indeed, the choice of Iran as the site of the conference pointed to the accordance given to the non-Western nations. Princess Ashraf Pahlavi, the twin sister of the Iranian leader, was president of the Human Rights Commission at the time and presided over the conference. Her brother, Reza Pahlavi, the shah of Iran, was an autocrat who was unwilling to implement democratic reforms, focusing instead on economic ones. In his welcoming speech to the conference delegates, the shah denounced several aspects of the Universal Declaration of Human Rights. Indeed, he proposed amending several aspects of the declaration to reflect less individual rights and more social and economic rights. "While we still revere the principles laid down in the Universal Declaration, it is nevertheless necessary to adjust them to the requirements of our time,"[5] said the shah.

Much to the chagrin of the Western delegates and others, the shah, in his speech, "denigrated the importance of political liberty, transforming human rights into social and economic entitlements. Rather than individual freedoms to be wielded against the power of the state, rights were bestowed by the regime and its development program,"[6] according to Burke. His sister, Princess Ashraf, later also dismissed the declaration as essentially outdated and encouraged the conference to consider an entirely new document.

As Burke notes, it became clear during the conference that a new perspective, which he calls "Third World rights ideology," had emerged. Led by the Iranians, supporters of this ideology valued social and economic rights above individual rights— the same argument that had been made in 1948 by the Soviet

In this March 1958 photo, Eleanor Roosevelt presents copies of *In Your Hands*, a guidebook of the U.S. observance of the tenth anniversary of the Universal Declaration of Human Rights, to Ambassador R.S.S. Gunawardene *(left)*, the newly elected chair of the UN Commission on Human Rights. Looking on is René Cassin.

members of the Human Rights Commission during the drafting of the declaration. Simply put, the overall economic prosperity of the nation took precedence over individual liberties. As one African delegate asked, "How can a poor people, physically, morally, and intellectually unhealthy, enjoy civil and political rights?"[7] Individual rights, such as freedom of speech, freedom of religion, and due process, were presented as luxuries that Western nations, being more financially stable, could afford to extend to their citizens. Less-developed, non-Western nations needed to focus instead on improving their economies.

Cassin, who was present at the Tehran conference, was outraged by the willingness of the non-Western delegates to dismiss outright the importance of individual rights. Many Western nations, including the United States, remained silent, realizing that because they no longer held the majority of the votes, their position would be easily defeated.

By the end of the conference on May 13, 1968, the majority of the members had adopted the Proclamation of Tehran (most of the Western states, of course, dissented). While the proclamation affirmed that "the Universal Declaration of Human Rights states a common understanding of the peoples of the world concerning the inalienable and inviolable rights of all members of the human family," it also stated that "the full realization of civil and political rights without the enjoyment of economic, social and cultural rights is impossible."[8] The proclamation stressed the importance of economic and social development of nations above all. Burke says, "For many, the conference outcome was somewhere between a failure and an outright catastrophe."[9] Its impact was palpable for the next 20 years, as economic concerns, rather than those pertaining to individual rights, guided the international human rights agenda.

VIENNA

Roland Burke notes, "Depressing for human rights scholars and embarrassing for the UN secretariat, Tehran has been cast

In 1978, the UN General Assembly commemorated the thirtieth anniversary of the Universal Declaration of Human Rights by presenting eight human rights awards, including one to Coretta Scott King *(standing)*, who received it on behalf of her late husband, Martin Luther King Jr.

aside for its much more glamorous and productive successor in Vienna."[10] In Vienna, much of the negativity toward the Universal Declaration of Human Rights was reversed, and the document's relevance to modern times upheld and affirmed.

In June 1993, the United Nations World Congress on Human Rights was held in Vienna, Austria. Seven thousand people, representing 171 countries and 800 nongovernmental organizations, participated. Described as an historic summit for human rights, the congress approved the Vienna Declaration and

(continues on page 96)

DIPLOMACY AND HUMAN RIGHTS

Since the Cold War ended, the issue of human rights has assumed a significant role in global diplomacy. In fact, even before the Soviet Union collapsed in 1991, it was becoming evident that human rights were being used as a way for nations to judge one another. For example, in 1975, the U.S. Congress mandated that it would not provide foreign aid to nations that were in severe violations of the human rights of their citizens. Two years later, President Jimmy Carter, a globally recognized advocate of human rights, declared that the issue of human rights was "the soul of U.S. foreign policy."*

One recent example of the impact of human rights in international diplomacy occurred prior to the 2008 Summer Olympics, held in Beijing, China. In 2001, it was announced by the Olympic committee that Beijing would host the summer Olympics, although it was stated that China should, in the intervening seven years, improve its human rights record, which according to all international monitors was dismal. For those who lived during those times, it is difficult to forget the Chinese government's crackdown on student demonstrators in Tiananmen Square in Beijing in 1989. The protestors had called for greater freedoms and rights, political and economic reform, and an end to the Communist government's many restrictive policies. The government, after several weeks, finally responded to the protests by sending troops and tanks into the square, an action that led to the deaths of an estimated 2,000 to 3,000 people (although the Chinese government's official number is much lower). In addition, ongoing problems in Tibet also cast a shadow on China's human rights record.

In March 2008, just a few months before the Olympics, Tibetan monks clashed with the Chinese police. (China has ruled Tibet since 1951; the small mountain nation has tried unsuccessfully to be liberated since.)

As the 2008 Olympics drew closer, many organizations and governments around the world insisted that China had not cleaned up its act. In 2006, the U.S. State Department issued a report in which it declared that China's record remained "poor." Specifically, it stated: "There was a trend towards increased harassment, detention, and imprisonment by government and security authorities of those perceived as threatening to government authority. The government also adopted measures to control more tightly print, broadcast and electronic media, and censored online content."**

The report also cited abuses in terms of fair trials, torture of prisoners, high rates of executions, and even reproductive rights. (China has a limit on the number of children a family may have as a way to curtail its booming population, which stands at 1.3 billion.) "The penalties for violating the law are strict," the report states, "leaving some women little choice but to abort pregnancies. . . . Reports of forced sterilizations and abortions, in violation of national law, continued to be documented in rural areas."****

In a report of its own, issued one day after the release of the U.S. report, the Chinese government listed human rights abuses committed by the United States against its own citizens and other people around the world, concluding that "the issue of human rights should become a theme of social development in all countries and of international cooperation, rather than a slogan for exporting ideologies or even a tool of diplomacy to fix others out of one's own political needs."***** The defensive tone of the Chinese

(continues)

(continued)
report indicated to many observers that its government was aware of increased international scrutiny immediately before the Olympics were set to take place. Despite calls from many countries and individuals for boycott of the Olympic Games, the games proceeded as usual.

---

* Robert G. Patman, ed. *Universal Human Rights?* New York: St. Martin's Press, 2000, p. 6.

** Jacqueline Langwith, ed. *Human Rights*. Detroit, Mich.: Greenhaven Press, 2008, p. 89.

*** Ibid., p. 100.

**** Ibid., p. 109.

(continued from page 93)

Programme of Action. The Vienna Declaration notes, among other things, "that the Universal Declaration of Human Rights, which constitutes a common standard of achievement for all peoples and all nations, is the source of inspiration and has been the basis for the United Nations in making advances."[11]

According to Robert G. Patman, the World Congress on Human Rights declared that "the promotion and protection of all human rights is a legitimate concern of the international community." In a response to the Proclamation of Tehran, the Vienna Declaration also states, "While the significance of national and regional particularities and various historical, cultural and religious backgrounds must be borne in mind, it is the duty of States, regardless of their political, economic and cultural systems, to promote and protect all human rights and fundamental freedoms."[12]

The congress also approved the establishment of a new position within the United Nations, that of the High Commissioner for Human Rights. José Ayala Lasso was nominated as the first high commissioner and assumed office a year after the conference. He was succeeded by Mary Robinson of Ireland in 1997, then by Sergio Vieira de Mello of Brazil, who served from 2002–2003. Canadian Louise Arbour served as high commissioner until 2008; Navanethem Pillay of South Africa has since succeeded her. The Office of the High Commissioner is part of the UN Secretariat and has its main office in Geneva, where it oversees human rights work and initiatives, as well as its branch offices around the world. It works closely with the Human Rights Commission of the United Nations, which was renamed the Human Rights Council in 2006.

In the 1990s, the United Nations also established the International Criminal Tribunal to try individuals who have been accused of human rights violations and crimes against humanity. (Because it was established in 2002, when the Rome Statute entered into force, it can only try crimes committed after that date.) Cases the tribunal has worked on include ones related to the genocide in Rwanda and to the killings in the former Yugoslavia, as well as cases relating to Darfur, Uganda, the Congo, and others.

10

Issues That Remain

WESTERN IDEALS

One of the major challenges the Universal Declaration of Human Rights has faced since the time of its drafting is the accusation from some countries that the rights presented are based on the values and ideals of Western nations, rather than on universal ones. Some point to the fact that many documents that influenced the drafting and wording of the declaration are foundational documents of Western governments, such as the U.S. Declaration of Independence and the French Declaration of the Rights of Man. Some also say that the values of freedom of speech, freedom of religion, and others derive from the ideas of the Enlightenment, the eighteenth-century Western intellectual and philosophical period in which reason was advocated as the only source for authority.

The main problem, critics says, is that Western values hold the rights of the individual above all else, including, in some cases, the security of the family and society. For non-Western nations and cultures that place emphasis on family, for example, the human rights listed in the declaration are problematic. Another example is the emphasis on rights that demonstrate a Western bias, such as the right to time off from work with pay. Shashi Tharoor, a longtime UN official, summarizes some of the opposing views to universal human rights (though he himself supports them) and says that the right to paid vacations is "always good for a laugh in the sweatshops of the developing world."[1]

Emerging or developing nations have usually leveled this charge of Western values against the declaration. Robert G. Patman writes, "A number of Third World countries took issue with what was seen as the UN's pro-Western focus on civil and political rights: it was economic, social and cultural rights, along with the right to self-determination and development which were generally seen as relevant to the needs and interests of most Third World nations."[2] In other words, it is the first set of rights—sometimes called "first-generation rights," which include freedoms of speech, religion, movement, and so on—that are problematic, because they are seen as taking priority over what are called the "second-generation rights" of housing, employment, health care, education, and other social and economic rights. For many emerging nations, however, establishing a sound economy, providing housing, and lifting people out of poverty are more important at this stage of their national history than an individual's rights to freedom of speech and thought.

The charge of the declaration as being infused with Western values was brought up even during its drafting in the late 1940s. It was rebutted by P.C. Chang, the Chinese representative on the Human Rights Commission. He challenged this argument by noting that the committee had surveyed a broad

President Bill Clinton presents the Eleanor Roosevelt Award for Human Rights to Tillie Black Bear, a Native American women's rights activist, on December 6, 2000. Roosevelt's name remains powerfully associated with the human rights cause.

range of human rights-related documents and that a number of perspectives were considered and included. Furthermore, the drafters included social and economic rights as a balance to the inclusion of individual civil and political rights.

Modern critics have challenged this idea that human rights are a Western concept as well. Faisal Kutty cites Malaysian politician and intellectual Anwar Ibrahim, who once wrote, "To say that freedom is western . . . is to offend our own traditions as well as our forefathers, who gave their lives in the struggle against tyranny and injustice."[3] Kutty adds that the notion that human rights are an exclusively Western concept is worse than just false—it is a "crutch used for so long by human rights violators."[4]

CULTURAL RELATIVISM

Related to the charge of Western values is that of cultural relativism. El Obaid Ahmed El Obaid neatly summarizes this position as advocating "that each and every culture has its own notion of human rights and freedoms. Human rights can only exist by reverting back to cultural norms, not looking to external (Western, legal) documents. Each group should look to their own culture to devise and implement their own notion of rights."[5]

In fact, proponents of this view sometimes hint that human rights are another form of Western imperialism and domination over the sovereignty of smaller, non-Western nations. This argument is also sometimes referred to as the "Asian values challenge," because many of its critics often come from Asian societies. A good illustration of this viewpoint, Fiona Boylan notes, is the one advocated in the late 1990s by the leaders of Singapore and Indonesia. They believed that the rights of the individual are not inherent in Asian culture and therefore should not be extended to people in that region.[6]

Another critic is Jieh-Yung Lo, who writes, "We should not all pursue human rights in the same way."[7] Lo points to the fact that global cultures differ from one another in terms of priorities and norms. While the freedoms of speech and religion are important in Western culture, they may not be as important in others. "Rather than focusing on individualism and democracy," he writes, "Asian values provide greater emphasis on the moral and collective duties of a human being . . . To sum it up, the community takes precedence over individuals, social and economic rights take precedence over civil and political rights, and rights themselves are a matter of national sovereignty."[8] Indeed, Lo's argument is reminiscent of the Soviet argument articulated by Vyshinsky and Pavlov in the 1940s, that rights should be dealt with on a nation-by-nation basis, and that a nation's sovereignty should prevent others from interfering in its domestic agenda.

Unsurprisingly, critics of the cultural relativism or "Asian values challenge" find this position to be dangerous. Boylan says, "If human rights are portrayed as culturally relative then they can be denied to certain groups."[9] The example of Nazi Germany is often used here to point out that a government can deem certain values inherent to its national culture and deny some segments of its population their rights; the Nazis claimed that the rights of Jews and other minorities had to be sacrificed for the prosperity of the nation. A report by Amnesty International on the fiftieth anniversary of the Universal Declaration of Human Rights found that "most governments who claim that the western tradition of individual rights is inimical [against] to their own culture do so to disguise their own political and economic interests."[10]

Tharoor makes the case against cultural relativism in a practical way: "There is nothing sacrosanct about culture anyway. Culture is constantly evolving in any living society, responding to both internal and external stimuli, and there is much in every culture that societies quite naturally outgrow and reject." To illustrate his point, he notes: "The fact that slavery was acceptable across the world for at least two thousand years does not make it acceptable to us now. . . . Coercion, not culture, is the test."[11] In other words, the victims of certain human rights violations—such as a young girl forced into a marriage or subjected to female castration—need simply be asked whether they agree with the violation because they accept it as part of their culture. If they do not agree with it, if they have been coerced into it, then a human rights violation has indeed occurred.

ISLAMIC FUNDAMENTALISM

In recent decades, Islamic fundamentalism has become one of the major issues on the world stage. In 1979, Islamic fundamentalists in Iran overthrew the more secular government and, under the leadership of the Ayatollah Ruhollah Khomeini, imposed strict Islamic law, sharia, on its citizens. As part of the global movement, some nations have either incorporated very harsh versions of sharia law into their national constitutions or strengthened sharia's influence on their legal systems.

Sharia law is based on three sources: the teachings in the Koran, the holy book of Islam; the Sunna, or the Islamic code of living as based on the sayings and teachings of the Prophet Muhammad; and the consensus of scholars of Islam. This law bans certain behaviors and actions as *haram*, or sinful, such as drinking alcohol, sexual intercourse outside of marriage, theft, and apostasy (leaving Islam to convert to another religion). There are many schools of sharia law, some more liberal than others, but the most conservative versions (which include flogging, stoning, or death for certain offenses) are being implemented in certain Islamic countries today.

Nations that support sharia view it as God's law and therefore believe it is sinful for humans to impose alternate systems of law in its place. Furthermore, its proponents argue that sharia law, being God's law, already accounts for and incorporates human rights into its system; they cite verses from the Koran and the Hadith, the book of the Prophet Muhammad's teachings, that state the equality of men and women, protect non-Muslims and guarantee their freedoms, and give other rights. They also argue that human rights, as formulated by the West, allow what they deem as inappropriate actions to be protected under the guise of rights. Louay M. Safi, an Islamic scholar, notes, "There are those who use human rights as a tool to reject non-western traditions, and therefore promote social ills, such as same-sex relations under the banner of human rights."[12]

Opponents of sharia, in both the Judeo-Christian West and in Islamic nations, criticize its implementation by arguing that it was developed in the early days of Islam and thus cannot be relevant to the needs and issues of the twenty-first century. They

(continues on page 106)

THE RIGHTS OF WOMEN IN ISLAMIC NATIONS

One of the most controversial human rights issues today is that of the rights of women in Islamic nations.

In many Western nations, Muslim women are portrayed in the media and popular culture as universally oppressed and silenced, subjected to violence in their home countries. While this is an overgeneralization, in some countries, such as Saudi Arabia, women are restricted in their actions; for example, a woman typically may not leave her home without a male escort, she must not be seen without a head covering, and she may not drive. Despite these rules, there are women's organizations in these nations that have tried to overturn these practices and restrictions.

In other countries, the crackdown on women's activities is relatively new and due in part to the emergence of a strong, fundamentalist Islamic movement. Stories that tend to shock Western observers include those in which women are stoned to death or killed in other ways for allegedly immoral behavior, such as committing adultery or engaging in sexual relationships outside of marriage. These are usually referred to as "honor killings," and while they occur rarely, they make headlines in the West when they do.

The most potent illustrations are nations like Afghanistan and Iran. In Afghanistan, writes Thomas M. Franck, "the Taliban's repression [of women] remains in a class by itself: denying women the right to leave home except when accompanied by a brother or husband and forbidding them all access to public education."* Public executions of women who have been accused of adultery—unheard of in modern Afghanistan before the rise of the Taliban government in the 1990s—have also taken place, usually with ceremonial fanfare before large crowds of people. In 2005, even after the Taliban was ousted from power by U.S.-led coalition forces, a 29-year-old woman was accused by her husband of committing adultery, after she apparently asked him for a legal separation. She was stoned to death by a gang of men, including her husband.

In Iran, the Islamic Revolution of 1979 caused a cultural uproar after strict interpretations of Islamic law were imposed on the population. While Iran is an advanced nation in many respects, a strict adherence to sharia law exists. When journalist Friedounce Sahebjam visited Iran, he learned of the particularly brutal execution of a local woman, whom he called Soraya M. (A film based on a book he wrote about the incident, *The Stoning of Soraya M.*, debuted in September 2008.) The victim had been falsely accused of adultery by her husband, who wanted to end their marriage so he could marry a younger woman; Soraya was buried in the ground up to her chest, then stoned to death by a mob that included her husband, two of her sons, and her own father.

Many Muslims feel that honor killings are overhyped in the West and are used to depict Islamic culture negatively. The problem, they say, is that Islamic countries are perceived as universally barbaric in their treatment of women, despite the fact that there are growing women's movements even in Islamic nations with the strictest sharia laws.

* Thomas M. Franck, "Are Human Rights Universal?" *Foreign Affairs* 80 (January/February 2001): p. 191.

(continued from page 103)
especially criticize its views on the rights of women and the individual rights of speech and religion. Azam Kamguian of the Committee to Defend Women's Rights in the Middle East writes, "In Iran, the Sudan, Pakistan and Afghanistan, Islamic regimes proceeded to transform women's homes into prison houses, where confinement of women, their exclusion from many fields of work and education, and their brutal treatment became the law of the land."[13] She points out that under sharia, a woman's testimony equals only half that of a man, which biases domestic cases in favor of the husband, and that in inheritance cases, sharia dictates that daughters inherit only half as much as sons.

Indeed, in countries like Afghanistan, where the Islamic fundamentalist Taliban regime ruled until it was overthrown by U.S.-led coalition forces in 2002, a woman could be convicted of adultery or other similar crimes of honor simply on hearsay testimony given to an Islamic court, and could be stoned to death or similarly executed in a public manner. Franck described one such example that occurred in the spring of 2000, in which "the Taliban . . . ordered a mother of seven to be stoned to death for adultery in front of an ecstatic stadium of men and children."[14]

In 1990, the Nineteenth Islamic Conference of Foreign Ministers in Cairo, Egypt, adopted the Cairo Declaration on Human Rights in Islam, which purported to establish a framework of human rights compatible with Islamic culture. The declaration opens by stating that the conference wished to affirm human rights in accordance with a lifestyle that adheres to sharia law; it also recognizes that "fundamental rights and universal freedoms in Islam are an integral part of the Islamic religion and that no one as a matter of principle has the right to suspend them in whole or in part or violate or ignore them in as much as they are binding divine commandments."[15]

While many of the rights articulated in the declaration establish the equality of men and women, Zehra F. Kabasakal Arat points out: "Some other articles of the Cairo Declaration also explicitly state that some rights and freedoms are recognized for men only. Article 12, for example, explicitly states that the freedoms of movement, selecting residence, and seeking asylum are reserved only for men."[16] Indeed, the document differentiates which rights are accorded to "everyone" or "every human being" and which are accorded to "every man."

CONCLUSION

In the end, the question remains: Has the Universal Declaration of Human Rights had any real effect on the human condition around the world?

The answer is "yes." The declaration, composed and created by a diverse group of voices hailing from China to Lebanon to the United States to France to Chile, demonstrated that people around the world could agree on common human rights and the notion that violating a person's rights should be neither justified nor dismissed. As Patman writes, "As well as serving as a source of hope for the downtrodden, the Declaration has also served as a reminder that the world should not turn a blind eye to the suffering of human beings regardless of frontiers."[17]

The declaration has also influenced more than 50 constitutions of emerging nations and many other regional covenants and treaties.[18] It has helped keep the flame alight for many human rights movements around the world. It has inspired voices that have risen in protest against the unjust treatment of people by governments, regimes, and individuals. Today, the anniversary of the adoption of the declaration, December 10, is observed worldwide as International Human Rights Day.

Nelson Mandela, who fought for and was imprisoned for more than a quarter century because of his advocacy of racial equality in South Africa, said of the power of the declaration: "The simple and noble words of the Universal Declaration were a sudden ray of hope at one of our darkest moments."[19] It cannot be denied that the declaration's role in inspiring and lifting up people around the world is very, very real.

CHRONOLOGY

1939   World War II begins; the Nazi regime in Germany
        conducts extermination program of Jews and
        other minorities.

1942   **January 1** The Declaration by United Nations is
        signed by the Allied Powers.

1945   **April 25** The United Nations Conference
        on International Organization is held in San
        Francisco, California.

        June 26 The United Nations Charter is approved.

TIMELINE

1939
World War II begins; the Nazi
regime in Germany conducts
extermination program of
Jews and other minorities.

December 10, 1948
The Universal Declaration of
Human Rights is approved
by the UN General Assembly.

1939

1948

August 14, 1945
World War II officially ends
with the Japanese surrender.

October 24, 1945
The United Nations Charter is ratified
and the UN comes into being.

August 14 World War II officially ends with the Japanese surrender.

October 24 The United Nations Charter is ratified and the UN comes into being.

1946   January 10 The first UN General Assembly meets in London, England; the Human Rights Commission is established.

1948   December 10 The Universal Declaration of Human Rights is approved by the UN General Assembly.

1961   July Amnesty International is founded.

July 1961
Amnesty
International
is founded.

1968
René Cassin
wins the Nobel
Peace Prize.

1994
The first High
Commissioner for
Human Rights is
appointed by the
United Nations.

1961

1994

June 1993
The World Conference on Human
Rights is held in Vienna, Austria.

1993
The first International Criminal Tribunal
is established in The Hague to deal with
war crimes in the former Yugoslavia.

1968	May The UN International Conference on Human Rights is held in Tehran, Iran.
	René Cassin wins the Nobel Peace Prize.
1971	Doctors Without Borders is founded.
1976	The International Covenant on Civil and Political Rights and the International Covenant on Economic, Social and Cultural Rights are ratified.
1978	Human Rights Watch is founded.
1993	June The World Conference on Human Rights is held in Vienna, Austria.
	The first International Criminal Tribunal is established in The Hague to deal with war crimes in the former Yugoslavia.
1994	The first High Commissioner for Human Rights is appointed by the United Nations.
2008	Amnesty International issues a major report on the status of human rights around the world 60 years after the Universal Declaration of Human Rights.

NOTES

CHAPTER 1

1. Lois Scharf, *Eleanor Roosevelt: First Lady of American Liberalism*. Boston: Twayne Publishers, 1987, p. 145.
2. Steve Neal, ed. "Eleanor and Harry: The Correspondence of Eleanor Roosevelt and Harry S. Truman." Truman Library. http://www.trumanlibrary.org/eleanor/1945.html.
3. Scharf, p. 145.
4. Ibid.
5. Ibid., p. 146.
6. Ibid., p. 147.

CHAPTER 2

1. Allida M. Black, *Casting Her Own Shadow: Eleanor Roosevelt and the Shaping of Postwar Liberalism*. New York: Columbia University Press, 1996, p. 1.
2. "Declaration by the United Nations, January 1, 1942." Avalon Project. http://avalon.law.yale.edu/20th_century/decade03.asp.
3. "United Nations Charter: Preamble, Purposes and Principles." UN Documents: Gathering a Body of Global Agreements. http://www.un-documents.net/ch-ppp.htm.
4. "Franklin Delano Roosevelt: *The Four Freedoms*." American Rhetoric. http://www.americanrhetoric.com/speeches/fdrthefourfreedoms.htm.
5. Chris Brown, "Universal Human Rights? An Analysis of the 'Human-rights Culture' and Its Critics," in *Universal Human Rights?*, ed. Robert G. Patman. New York: St. Martin's Press, 2000, p. 37.
6. Mary Ann Glendon, *A World Made New: Eleanor Roosevelt and the Universal Declaration of Human Rights*. New York: Random House, 2001, pp. 55–56.

CHAPTER 3

1. Scharf, p. viii.
2. Ibid., p. 17.
3. Ibid., p. 18.
4. Ibid.
5. Ibid., p. 27.
6. Ibid., p. 29.
7. Ibid., p. 47.
8. Black, p. 1.
9. Glendon, p. 35.

CHAPTER 4

1. Glendon, p. 45.
2. Ibid., p. 47.
3. Ibid., p. 48.
4. Ibid., p. 50.
5. Charles Malik, "What Are Human Rights?" Universal Declaration of Human Rights 50th Anniversary. http://www.udhr.org/history/whatare.htm.
6. Glendon, p. 48.

CHAPTER 5

1. Glendon, p. 56.
2. Ibid., pp. 271–274.

3. Ibid., p. 58.

4. "Magna Carta," in *The Human Rights Reader: Major Political Essays, Speeches, and Documents from Ancient Times to the Present*, 2nd ed., ed. Micheline R. Ishay. New York: Routledge, 2007, p. 483.

5. Ibid., p. 484.

6. "The United States Declaration of Independence (1776)," in *The Human Rights Reader: Major Political Essays, Speeches, and Documents from Ancient Times to the Present*, 2nd ed., ed. Micheline R. Ishay. New York: Routledge, 2007, p. 488.

7. Ibid., p. 489.

8. "United States Constitution: Bill of Rights." Cornell University Law School. http://www.law.cornell.edu/constitution/constitution.billofrights.html.

9. "The French Declaration of the Rights of Man and Citizen, (1789)," in *The Human Rights Reader: Major Political Essays, Speeches, and Documents from Ancient Times to the Present*, 2nd ed., ed. Micheline R. Ishay. New York: Routledge, 2007, p. 490.

10. Glendon, p. 38.

11. Ibid., p. 60.

12. Ibid., p. 63.

13. Ibid., p. 64.

14. "John Humphrey: A Profile." America—Engaging the World. http://www.america.gov/st/hr-english/2008/October/20081023144159emsutfol0.5762095.html.

15. Glendon, p. 274.

CHAPTER 6

1. Glendon, p. 69.

2. Ibid., p. 79.

3. Ibid., p. 90.

4. Ibid., pp. 97–98.

5. Ibid., p. 138.

CHAPTER 7

1. Glendon, p. 107.

2. Ibid., p. 114.

3. Ibid., p. 112.

4. Ibid., p. 113.

5. Ibid., p. 124.

6. Ibid., p. 139.

7. Ibid., p. 143.

8. Ibid., p. 151.

9. Ibid., p. 161.

CHAPTER 8

1. Glendon, p. 164.

2. Ibid., pp. 166–167.

3. Scharf, p. 148.

4. "Charles Malik Biography." Universal Declaration of Human Rights 50th Anniversary. http://www.udhr.org/history/Biographies/biocm.htm.

5. Glendon, p. 193.

6. Scharf, p. 148.

7. "Presentation Speech." Nobelprize.org. http://nobelprize.org/nobel_prizes/peace/laureates/1968/press.html.

8. "René Cassin: The Nobel Peace Prize 1968." Nobelprize.org. http://nobelprize.org/nobel_prizes/peace/laureates/1968/cassin-bio.html.

9. Robert G. Patman, ed., *Universal Human Rights?* New York: St. Martin's Press, 2000, p. 2.

10. Jacqueline Langwith, ed. *Human Rights*. Detroit, Mich.: Greenhaven Press, 2008, p. 14.

11. Patman, p. 6.

12. "Who We Are." Amnesty International. http://www.amnesty.org/en/who-we-are.

13. Patman, p. 10.

14. "About Us." Human Rights Watch. http://www.hrw.org/en/about.

15. "About Us: History and Principles." Doctors Without Borders. http://doctorswithout borders.org/aboutus/?ref= main-menu.

CHAPTER 9

1. Glendon, p. 170.

2. Langwith, p. 15.

3. Roland Burke, "From Individual Rights to National Development: The First UN International Conference on Human Rights, Tehran, 1968," *Journal of World History*, Vol. 19, No. 3, September 2008, p. 276.

4. Burke, p. 277.

5. Ibid., p. 284.

6. Ibid.

7. Ibid., p. 295.

8. "Proclamation of Teheran." Office of the High Commissioner for Human Rights. http://www.unhchr.ch/html/menu3/b/b_tehern.htm.

9. Burke, p. 276.

10. Ibid.

11. "Vienna Declaration and Programme of Action." Office of the High Commissioner for Human Rights. http://

www.unhchr.ch/huridocda/huridoca.nsf/(Symbol)/A.CONF.157.23.En?Open Document.

12. Ibid.

CHAPTER 10

1. Shashi Tharoor, "Are Human Rights Universal?" *World Policy Journal* 26 (Winter 1999/2000). http://www.worldpolicy.org/journal/tharoor.html.

2. Patman, p. 4.

3. Langwith, p. 46.

4. Ibid., p. 47.

5. Ibid., p. 38.

6. Boylan, p. 24.

7. Langwith, p. 35.

8. Ibid., p. 33.

9. Ibid., p. 30.

10. Janna Palmer, "Hollow Celebration of 50 Years of Human-rights Campaigning," *Lancet* 351 (June 27, 1998): p. 1940.

11. Tharoor.

12. Langwith, p. 81.

13. Ibid., p. 73.

14. Thomas M. Franck, "Are Human Rights Universal?" *Foreign Affairs* 80 (January/February 2001): p. 191.

15. "The Cairo Declaration on Human Rights in Islam." Religion and Law: International Document Database. http://www.religlaw.org/interdocs/docs/cairohrislam1990.htm.

16. Zehra F. Kabasakal Arat, "Forging a Global Culture of Human Rights: Origins and Prospects of the International Bill of

Rights," *Human Rights Quarterly* 28 (2006): p. 433.

17. Patman, pp. 15–16.

18. Jerome Shestack, "Review of *The Universal Declaration of Human Rights: Origins, Drafting, and Intent*, by Johannes Morsink," *American Journal of International Law* 94 (2000): p. 600.

19. Mary Robinson, "The Universal Declaration of Human Rights: A Living Document." Keynote address to Symposium on Human Rights in the Asia-Pacific Region, Tokyo, Japan, January 27, 1998. Reprinted in *Australian Journal of International Affairs* 52 (July 1998): p. 119.

BIBLIOGRAPHY

"About Us: History and Principles," Doctors Without Borders. Available online. URL: http://doctorswithoutborders.org/aboutus/?ref=main-menu.

"About Us," Human Rights Watch. Available online. URL: http://www.hrw.org/en/about.

Arat, Zehra F. Kabasakal. "Forging a Global Culture of Human Rights: Origins and Prospects of the International Bill of Rights." *Human Rights Quarterly* 28 (2006).

Black, Allida M. *Casting Her Own Shadow: Eleanor Roosevelt and the Shaping of Postwar Liberalism*. New York: Columbia University Press, 1996.

Brown, Chris. "Universal Human Rights? An Analysis of the 'Human-rights Culture' and Its Critics." In *Universal Human Rights?*, ed. Robert G. Patman. New York: St. Martin's Press, 2000.

"The Cairo Declaration on Human Rights in Islam," Religion and Law: International Document Database. Available online. URL: http://www.religlaw.org/interdocs/docs/cairohrislam1990.htm.

"Charles Malik Biography," Universal Declaration of Human Rights 50th Anniversary. Available online. URL: http://www.udhr.org/history/Biographies/biocm.htm.

"Declaration by the United Nations, January 1, 1942," Avalon Project. Available online. URL: http://avalon.law.yale.edu/20th_century/decade03.asp.

Franck, Thomas M. "Are Human Rights Universal?" *Foreign Affairs* 80 (January/February 2001).

"Franklin Delano Roosevelt: The Four Freedoms," American Rhetoric. Available online. URL: http://www.americanrhetoric.com/speeches/fdrthefourfreedoms.htm.

Freedman, Russell. *Eleanor Roosevelt: A Life of Discovery*. New York: Clarion Books, 1997.

"The French Declaration of the Rights of Man and Citizen (1789)." In *The Human Rights Reader: Major Political Essays, Speeches, and Documents from Ancient Times to the Present*. 2nd ed., ed. by Micheline R. Ishay. New York: Routledge, 2007.

Glendon, Mary Ann. *A World Made New: Eleanor Roosevelt and the Universal Declaration of Human Rights*. New York: Random House, 2001.

"John Humphrey: A Profile," America.gov. Available online. URL: http://www.america.gov/st/hrenglish/2008/October/20081023144159emsutfol0.5762095.html.

"Magna Carta." In *The Human Rights Reader: Major Political Essays, Speeches, and Documents from Ancient Times to the Present*. 2nd ed., ed. by Micheline R. Ishay. New York: Routledge, 2007.

Malik, Charles. "What Are Human Rights?" Universal Declaration of Human Rights 50th Anniversary. Available online. URL: http://www.udhr.org/history/whatare.htm.

Neal, Steve, ed. "Eleanor and Harry: The Correspondence of Eleanor Roosevelt and Harry S. Truman," Truman Library. Available online. URL: http://www.trumanlibrary.org/eleanor/1945.html.

Palmer, Janna. "Hollow Celebration of 50 Years of Human-rights Campaigning." *Lancet* 351 (June 27, 1998).

Patman, Robert G., ed. *Universal Human Rights?* New York: St. Martin's Press, 2000.

"Presentation Speech," Nobelprize.org. Available online. URL: http://nobelprize.org/nobel_prizes/peace/laureates/1968/ press.html.

"Proclamation of Teheran," Office of the High Commissioner for Human Rights. Available online. URL: http://www. unhchr.ch/html/menu3/b/b_tehern.htm.

"René Cassin: The Nobel Peace Prize 1968," Nobelprize.org. Available online. URL: http://nobelprize.org/nobel_prizes/ peace/laureates/1968/cassin-bio.html.

Robinson, Mary. "The Universal Declaration of Human Rights: A Living Document." Keynote address to Symposium on Human Rights in the Asia-Pacific Region, Tokyo, Japan, January 27, 1998. Reprinted in *Australian Journal of International Affairs* 52 (July 1998).

Scharf, Lois. *Eleanor Roosevelt: First Lady of American Liberalism*. Boston: Twayne Publishers, 1987.

Shestack, Jerome. "Review of *The Universal Declaration of Human Rights: Origins, Drafting, and Intent*, by Johannes Morsink." *American Journal of International Law* 94 (2000).

Tharoor, Shashi. "Are Human Rights Universal?" *World Policy Journal* 26 (Winter 1999/2000).

"United Nations Charter: Preamble, Purposes and Principles," UN Documents: Gathering a Body of Global Agreements. Available online. URL: http://www.un-documents.net/ch-ppp.htm.

"United States Constitution: Bill of Rights," Cornell University Law School. Available online. URL: http://www.law.cornell. edu/constitution/constitution.billofrights.html.

"The United States Declaration of Independence (1776)." In *The Human Rights Reader: Major Political Essays, Speeches, and Documents from Ancient Times to the Present*. 2nd ed., edited by Micheline R. Ishay. New York: Routledge, 2007.

"Vienna Declaration and Programme of Action," Office of the High Commissioner for Human Rights. Available online. URL: http://www.unhchr.ch/huridocda/huridoca.nsf/ (Symbol)/A.CONF.157.23.En?OpenDocument.

"Who We Are," Amnesty International. Available online. URL: http://www.amnesty.org/en/who-we-are.

FURTHER RESOURCES

BOOKS

Amnesty International. *We Are All Born Free: The Universal Declaration of Human Rights in Pictures*. London: Frances Lincoln Children's Books, 2008.

Hubbard-Brown, Janet. *Eleanor Roosevelt: First Lady*. New York: Chelsea House, 2008.

National Geographic. *Every Human Has Rights: What You Need to Know About Your Human Rights*. Foreword by Mary Robinson. Des Moines, Iowa: National Geographic Children's Books, 2008.

Rocha, Ruth, and Otavio Roth. *Universal Declaration of Human Rights: An Adaptation for Children*. New York: United Nations Publications, 1990.

WEB SITES

Human Rights. U.S. Department of State
http://www.state.gov/g/drl/hr

Office of the High Commissioner for Human Rights, United Nations
http://www.ohchr.org/EN/Pages/WelcomePage.aspx

The Universal Declaration of Human Rights, United Nations
http://www.un.org/Overview/rights.html

PICTURE CREDITS

INDEX

ABOUT THE AUTHOR

SUSAN MUADDI DARRAJ is an associate professor of English at Harford Community College in Bel Air, Maryland. She has written several titles for Chelsea House. She is senior editor of the *Baltimore Review*, a literary journal that publishes fiction, nonfiction, poetry, and book reviews. She lives in Baltimore, Maryland.